Between the Atlantic and the Mediterranean

Responses to Climate and Weather Conditions throughout History

Edited by Cristina Joanaz de Melo, Ana Isabel Queiroz, Luís Espinha da Silveira and Ian D. Rotherham

Proceedings of the conference held at Faculdade de Ciências Sociais e Humanas, Universidade NOVA de Lisboa, Lisbon, 4th-5th May 2012

Edited by Cristina Joanaz de Melo, Ana Isabel Queiroz, Luís Espinha da Silveira and Ian D. Rotherham.

ISBN 978-1-904098-53-9

Published by:
Wildtrack Publishing,
Venture House,
103 Arundel Street,
Sheffield S1 2NT
UK

Typeset and processed by Christine Handley

Front cover photograph: *Quercus faginae* woodland, Arrábida Natural Park Portugal.
© Luis Silveira.

Table of contents

Introduction

Cristina Joanaz de Melo, Ana Isabel Queiroz, Luís Espinha da Silveira

Between the Atlantic and the Mediterranean: Responses to Climate and Weather Conditions throughout History brings together a set of case studies on living organisms' adaptation to the evolution of the climate and adjustments to extreme weather conditions.

Aiming to go beyond concerns about recent and forthcoming climate change, which have dominated research in environmental studies, but without excluding them, this book adopts a long-term perspective on the adaptations and adjustments to nature. Although an important group of papers deal with the Portuguese territory and the Iberian Peninsula, in which a complex mosaic of Atlantic and Mediterranean climates helped to shape landscapes and history, the book has a broader geographical scope from England, on one side to Italy, on the other. Overall, it aims to offer new contributions looking at the distribution and numbers of animal species and, material, social, cultural and religious responses to weather in the short term and to climate in the long term.

The common ground for the analyses is the reaction of living organisms to what we would call today "natural hazards". In the long term, these are cyclical, and nowadays predictable.

The book which is, underpinned by environmental history, presents a holistic vision of the subject. It establishes a dialogue with other fields of knowledge within the humanities (geography, history of religion, and archaeology) and the natural sciences (ecology and biogeography) providing a multilayered interdisciplinary approach to the analysis.

The present book is in four sections reflected by the following headings:

1. **Erosion and population:** how society deals with the erosion effects and responses to changed landscapes;
2. **Space and climate**: how species' distribution and life history evolved in relation to climate changing conditions;

3. **Human responses to weather - building and praying**: how humans react in response to natural hazards by building hard defences and calling for divine protection;
4. **Imagined landscapes**: how the way that weather and landscape are portrayed in literature and influences perceptions of the territory and, at the same time, how those perceptions are influenced by feelings, experiences and values.

The first section opens with Agnoletti's analysis of the progressive development of State policy in Italy in the nineteenth and twentieth centuries to prevent erosion through the afforestation and restoration of mountain watersheds. To explain the modest results which were made up to the Second World War he refers not only to the economic and social obstacles that such a policy had to face but also to the technical and scientific disagreements within the Italian forestry school regarding the measures to be taken.

Considering a different type of landscape, the plains and small hills in the south of Portugal, Roxo brings to our attention the dramatic soil erosion caused by a State policy adopted in the last decades of the nineteenth century and lasting until the middle of the twentieth century. Here, the State policy was directed towards increasing cereal production. The expansion of production into areas with low fertility soils, combined with heavy rains and land mismanagement was responsible for enduring land degradation.

Results from pollen and charcoal analyses have questioned the assumption that environmental conditions ruled the economy and society of the prehistoric and medieval mobile human communities in Mediterranean mountains. This is the argument that Moreno-Garcia and Pimenta present in their chapter, which starts the second section. They show that open summer grazing areas in the highest points of the mountains, which support mobile pastoral systems, are a consequence rather of extensive woodland clearance. Seasonal grazing which has maintained these secondary habitats over time has followed this.

The work by Harris is underpinned by biogeography. He looks, therefore, at the long-term scale that makes up periodic climatic changes, which have occurred during the Quaternary. He uses genetics, field data and modelling techniques to explain why the Iberian Peninsula is a hotspot of biodiversity. Among other examples, his text highlights the endemic salamander *Chioglossa lusitanica*, which currently inhabits only "refuge areas" in the centre and north-western parts of Portugal.

As in other European countries increases in rainfall and consequently in severe flooding in nineteenth-century Portugal, triggered the need for environmental policies to prevent natural hazards. However, effective solutions to alleviate storms and torrential floods were repeatedly debated in Parliament and it was only in 1884 that the first national regulations were passed. While politicians were discussing the limits of State intervention in private properties, local populations across the country developed their own strategies to protect themselves. The rights of utilisation of commonland, moors and heaths, which were not privately owned, furnished them with materials to survive. The materials were adequate to build walls or small dams to sustain river margins, provided shrubs to make cabanas (shelters), and stone or wood to make tools or personal equipment to shelter people, cattle and machinery from the unexpected extreme weather conditions. This way, Melo argues, the exploitation of materials with low economic values, from poor landscapes was turned into a profitable activity.

When human communities were unable to deal with the disruptive character of weather events they would appeal to transcendent protection. In this chapter, Picoito presents a study of medieval and early modern cyclical and solstice rites as well as commemorative and piacular rites, "extraordinary requests for help made to saints, images or relics". These rites resulted from the Christianisation of popular (folk or local cultural) religion, a process where the Church struggled to dominate time, space, rituals, and objects. These were all mobilised by the folk culture in order to guarantee supernatural protection against natural threats.

Novels and fiction inspire people's perceptions about beautiful, frightening, heavenly or evil landscapes. Queiroz analyses the stories by the Portuguese writers Miguel Torga and Ferreira de Castro from the 1940s. In their writings, chilly and windy conditions encountered in the highest mountains are portrayed as unbearable, causing misery and suffering to the poor mountaineers. As time went on, she argues, changes in the socio-economic and political setting altered the harsh way people perceived the poor weather. Recently tourism and wind energy have started to develop and local communities have been profiting from what were formerly severe living conditions.

For centuries wetlands were places to avoid, being associated with evil and raising feelings of fear and loathing. Writers helped to create images of these landscapes, but there were also both myth and popular culture behind those perceptions. As Rotherham explains, “today, contemporary landscapes of heaths, commons, moors, bogs and fens are often places to visit and to recreate […]. Frequently our images and expectations are based not on direct experience, but on observations, imaginations and writings of earlier visitors and commentators.” Understanding the reactions of people to these fearful landscapes is important in promoting tourism, he argues.

To conclude, the contribution of this book lays in the diversity of the geographic scales of analysis, in the adoption of different time-frames and in the collaboration among various disciplines with their own sources and methods. This allows for diverse approaches to a rich and multifaceted subject that is at the centre of current research and occupies a prominent place among the concerns of society today.

Watershed management and afforestation between the nineteenth and twentieth centuries in Italy

Mauro Agnoletti,

Universita di Firenze

Abstract

The reforestation and restoration of mountain watersheds represent the most important and problematic commitment of the Amministrazione Forestale [Italian Forestry Authority] to date. The reasons for it has not much to do with the climatic situation of the period, but mostly with the effect of a socioeconomic situation characterized by a fast demographic growth, the need of farmed land, energy sources and timber. The purpose of restoring the hydrogeological damage to Italy's mountains was, however, subject to conflicting pressures. These related to the evolution of political tendencies, to social and economic factors and to the technical guidance for the work carried out, which hindered the achievement of significant results at least until the Second World War.

During the period considered, the maturation of a different political culture in terms of state intervention is observed. This developed in tandem with deep scientific thinking within the Italian forestry school in search of a better adaptation of its technical and scientific guidance to the problems of erosion control. From a period of a reduced intervention of the state, from 1869 until 1910, a growing public commitment can be observed with a peak of the state expenditures during the fascism, when also the most important laws for forest protection and land reclamation were enacted.

The factors involved and the large amount of documentary material available deserve a more detailed study, chronologically and geographically diversified, which goes far beyond the scope of this short essay based on the analysis of relevant forestry literature. Therefore, only some aspects of the problem are taken into account. This problem is characterised by an extraordinary continuity given the impressive sequence of landslides and floods that characterise the history of Italy and the still ongoing debate on intervention strategies.

Keywords: Erosion, forest, forestation, forestry engineering, restoration, watersheds, woods

Between economic liberalism and environmental emergencies: recognition of the role of the woods and the first operational interventions

The problem of erosion control and the importance of maintaining and expanding the woods for erosion control were already present in the legislation of the Italian states of the pre-unification period. However, it took a few years for it to be recognised as being of importance and to develop policy to adjust the matter at national level[i]. Attempts to unify forest legislation began in 1862 with the first project by Minister Pepoli, which was followed by others over the next ten years, including that of Minister Finali in 1873. These were initiatives, however, which did not recommend much for the use of the forest as a means to protect against hydrogeological damage. In addition, little relevance was given to the 1874 law on municipal uncultivated property, which compelled municipalities to reforest or transfer fallow land to third parties for them to reforest because the municipalities had no funds and few were interested in buying the land. Even the direct intervention of the state was modest, albeit with initiatives which included a limited financial commitment: the first free distribution of seedlings for reforestation, which occurred in 1873, gave only 148,000 seedlings coming from as few as ten forest nurseries located throughout the national territory.

The first measures of note were recorded in 1867, when the provincial council of Cuneo allocated an amount of 2000 lire for reforestation work, to which was added an equivalent sum from the Ministry of Agriculture. This represented the starting point for the establishment of the first consortium between the state and a province on a continuous basis. Formalised by a decree in 1872, this established a Forestry Committee with the purpose of designating the deforested and ploughed land that "affected the course of the waters and produced damage" and to provide for reforestation[ii]. Reforestation consortia were the most important entities dedicated to this activity and it is due to their efforts that most of the works were carried out up to the beginning of the 1900s. At least until the 1877

---

[i] For the latest news on forestry restrictions before the unification see Trifone, R., (1953) *Il vincolo forestale prima e dopo la legge del 1877*, Annali dell'Accademia Italiana di Scienze Forestali, 1, 61-76.

[ii] The Forestry Committee is an entity that also appears in the subsequent legislative measures. It consisted of the prefect of the province, the inspector of the Ripartimento Forestale [Forest Department], one engineer of the Genio Civile Provinciale, two members of the Deputazione Provinciale [Provincial Delegation], and two other members chosen from outside the Delegation, having heard the Agricultural Committees of the Province. The management of reforestation works was entrusted to the forest inspector. Cfr. MAIC, (1915) *Relazione sull'Azienda del Demanio Forestale di Stato*, Rome, 233-235.

law, however, they represented the result of special agreements between the State and the provinces concerned, while the new measure would explicitly promote the Constitution.

A major turning point came therefore with the 1877 law, which established in its principles the importance of the woods for water drainage and imposed *vincolo forestale* [the prohibition of removing a forest]. This was the moment when the 1923 law called "hydrogeological *vincolo*" was established where the woods were defended in terms of their protective function. The law accepted the upper limit of the chestnut grove for the imposition of the *vincolo*, in practice by dividing the mountain into two areas with different regimes in this respect. In the upper area deforestation was prohibited in the lower area it could allowed.This introduced several amendments and exceptions to Minister Finali's project which were more restrictive, allowing only the *vincolo* regarding the conservation of land and the water regime[iii]. A great emphasis has been recently given in the environmental history literature to the role of John Perkins Marsh for promoting this law[iv]. However, despite his friendship with Adolfe De Berenger, the director of the First Italian forest school created in Vallambrosa, near Florence, in 1869 and the long period of time spent there, there is no reference to him or his book "Man and Nature" in the forest literature of the period. Considering his role of American Ambassador in Italy, Marsh had probably some influence at political level in Rome and was not involved in any scientific debate about afforestation and watershed management.

Both contemporary sources and recent historiographical literature interpret the law as the result of a policy of liberal inspiration, which tended to favour private property and limit state intervention in the conservation of the woods. A trend became clear in 1869 when, despite the establishment of the forest school of Vallombrosa (the first Italian school of forestry founded near Florence in Tuscany), there was an attempt to dispose of all state forests forfeited by the State in Tuscany. This was opposed by the then Secretary General of the Ministry, Luzzatti, who then secured the establishment of the first state forestry domains.

[iii] In the first area the restriction was to be the rule and in the second there was to be one exception but in fact the list of exceptions in both areas was such that discrete margins of freedom were allowed to private individuals. Cfr. Osti, G. (1913) *Appunti per uno studio sistematico della legislazione forestale, «L'Alpe»,* 3-5, 83-89.

[iv] According to Marcus Hall J.P. Marsh played an important role in promoting the law at political level and his book was very popular among managers and adminstrators. M.Hall, Earth Repair. A transatlantic History of Environmental Restoration, University of Virginia Press, Charlottensville and London, 2005. 44-51.

The heated controversy over the legitimacy of the *vincolo*, which anticipated and followed the promulgation of the law, through which the Tuscan ultraliberals distinguished themselves voting against , should not therefore be misleading. Because in reality the law does not reduce but extends the freedom of individuals following the idea of "getting rid of laws inspired by principles of protectionism from other times" already corroborated in Parliament in 1874. The measure limited interventions to land with *vincolo*, allowing great freedom for private clearance especially in the lower range of the chestnut groves where the imposition of the *vincolo* assumed the character of exceptions. Moreover, the choice of the limit of the chestnut evidently immediately gave rise to different interpretations and notable differences as this species can grow from sea level up to 1500m above sea level with substantial differences from the north to the south of Italy. Although the regulations did tackle this problem by trying to limit these difficulties, it remained a constant source of uncertainty.

The director of the Istituto Forestale di Vallambrosa [Forest Institute], Adolfo di Berenger, who had been working on the draft law up to 1869 on behalf of the Minister of Agriculture Minghetti, immediately opposed the new law. Imagining that his claims were not being taken into due account, Di Berenger openly expressed his disagreement and because of this was prematurely put into retirement via an order by Minister Majorana Calatabiano. This provoked a strong impression in the forestry world.

However, such a measure could not strengthen the content of the law. The type of *vincoli* imposed both on the woods and on denuded land soon proved ineffective. It did not call for a real development of the activity of reforestation as both the expropriation and the creation of consortia between the State, the provinces and private individuals went on very slowly. Likewise the work of "lavori di sistemazione"["watershed restoration] which could be financed by an amount equal to 65% of the total had limited development, as it only left the majority of those concerned with the choice of constituting a consortium. The inadequacy of the law was confirmed by the subsequent parliamentary initiatives aimed at changing it, such as Minister Berti's bill in 1882 with the significant title "Provisions to promote reforestation"[v]. It was not until 1888 that a legislative measure was approved to recognise the authority of the Ministry of Agriculture to decide which land was for reforestation or for restoration through special projects prepared by the Amministrazione

---

[v] Trifone, R., (1957) Storia del diritto forestale in Italia cit., **180**.

Forestale [Forestry Administration]. The 1888 measure was seen positively by some foresters who saw in this restriction a strong limitation to development, exclusive to land with *vincoli*, and believed that the new law would give Italy parity with nations such as France, which had enacted a law on the subject as early as 1860. Nevertheless, these hopes were soon dashed and six reform projects were presented to Parliament up until 1910 in order to eliminate the drawbacks of a legal system judged excessive. This was in part due to the strict prohibitions it imposed and insufficient in part because of its narrow view.

In the period between 1867 and 1888, the effectiveness of the 1877 law was minimal with regard to the execution of large-scale works, and the twelve consortia established in this period only reforested 7,383 hectares. The most important reforestations were those in the province of Genoa, mainly with maritime pine (*Pinus pinaster*), Aleppo pine (*Pinus halepensis*) and larch pine (*Pinus laricio*) which were extended over 3,522 ha, and the reforestation in Aquila of 1,480 ha. Whilst the most important works of restoration were the ones undertaken in the province of Sondrio. The preference given to conifers was due to the need to employ species with reduced ecological requirements that could grow in poor top soil, often compacted from the effects of grazing and degraded by the passage of fire. These conditions, did not allow the immediate use of broadleaf trees. Some critics to this choice, not favouring natural species, does not take into account that the degraded soil would not allow the direct plantation of a beech or an oak forest which, as climax forests, come at the final stage of ecological evolution[vi]. A problem the any forester of that period was aware of. Obviously the growing dependence of Italy on imported timber, also supported the hope of having forests useful for the production of timber, a secondary objective of afforestation for which Italy was lacking, according to indications from the Amministrazione Forestale in terms of silviculture. Obviously the growing dependence of Italy on imported timber, also supported the hope of having forests useful for the production of timber, a secondary objective of afforestation for which Italy was lacking, according to indications from the Amministrazione Forestale in terms of silviculture[vii].

[vi] M.Armiero, A rugged nation, Mountains and the Making of Modern Italy. Cambridge: The White Horse Press, 2011.

[vii] On the need to expand the conifers see: (1885)*Le principali foreste d'Italia*, «Nuova Rivista Forestale», VIII. For a general evaluation of the problem of timber in Italy see: Agnoletti, M., (1999) *Foreste e industria del legno dall'Unità d'Italia al ventennio fascista*, in: SEHA-Departamento de historia e instituciones economicas UPV/EHU, IX Congress of Agrarian History, Zarautz, 707-720.

Despite the limited results, the 1888 law showed a change in State policy and in the guiding concepts of its intervention because it acknowledged the substantial ineffectiveness of an attitude that limited the initiative of the public administration in this matter. The subsequent measures of 1893, the law on land reclamation of 1900, which also covered reforestation, and the following special measures for the southern regions must be interpreted in this light. This change in the philosophy of the State culminated in the law of June 2, 1910, no. 277 which, by establishing the State Forests Domain, favoured reforestation and restoration. It gave the public company of the State Forests Domain funds and included expertise for the organisation of reforestation consortia. This was followed by the law of July 13, 1911, no. 774 where the first two sections show steps toward the hydraulic restoration of mountain watersheds and later transformed into a separate text promulgated with a R.D. [diploma with the same value as a decree] of March 21, 1912, no. 442. Here it clearly stated that both the link between the forest management of mountain watersheds and the hydrological restoration of rivers, including the need for a strong State initiative to implement the works, was adopted for the first time with the wording "hydrological and forest". This did not appear in the 1877 law[viii]. It was established that restoration and reforestation works would be made "by and at the expense of the State", as well as taking temporary surrender of private funds for the execution of reforestation. The expropriation for reasons of public utility was a different measure because the owner had the right to recover funds but had the obligation of managing land according to the plan of cultivation and conservation, and could not give the land up for it to be purchased by the State.

Analysis of the interventions carried out between 1888 and 1912 shows a slightly better situation than before. In this period, 16,826 hectares were reforested, and the number of consortia in 1910-11 had risen to twenty-six. In 1886, the number of forest nurseries had reached 32. As an effect of the law of June 2, 1910, they reached 168 spread between 35 provinces of the kingdom, on state-owned, municipal, private and leased land. This still had many planning flaws. The growth led to a rise in the distribution of free seedlings to private and municipal owners which, from a number below one million, in 1877-78,

---

[viii] The laws enacted were: law of June, 26, 1902 no. 245 on the Puglia aqueduct; law of March, 31, 1904 no. 140 on the Basilicata; law of July, 19, 1906 no. 390, on the damages from the eruption of the Vesuvio; law of June, 25, 1906 no. 255 on Calabria; Osti, G. (1913) *Appunti per uno studio sistematico della legislazione forestale, «L'Alpe», 3-5,* pp.87-89, and Carullo, F. (1951) *La sistemazione idraulico-forestale dei bacini montani e leggi 10 Agosto 1950, n 646 e 647*, «L'Italia Forestale e Montana», 5, 217-231.

increased to about 30 million in 1912-13. Beyond that, there was an increase of almost 100% between 1910 and 1914; and a rise to almost 130 million between 1912 and 1922[ix].

Reforestation and social and economic factors: the reasons for defeat

Compared to the estimates of the Amministrazione Forestale, which indicated an urgent need to reforest at least 400,000 hectares, it is clear that the results obtained in this first period were very modest. However, the assessment of the reduced effectiveness of State intervention must take into account the context of a range of social and economic factors that the action to restructure with which the Italian mountains had to contend. Chief among these was undoubtedly the increase in population, which saw numbers double between 1861 and 1925 resulting immediately in a true "assault to the mountain" greater than has been described for other European areas[x]. A phenomenon that was unparalleled in modern times, affecting the entire national territory and increasing the mountain population from about 5,000,000 to 8,500,000 inhabitants by 1925[xi].

This increase did not occur in a uniform manner across various parts of Italy, assuming different rates of growth, but it had major consequences in terms of the forest. The same foresters did not fail to denounce this lack of uniformity[xii]. The need for new arable land was not solved by an increase in unit production through technological development but rather with the extension of the cultivated area. This also affected the marginal areas

---

[ix] Many kilograms of seeds were also distributed. The increase in the number of seedlings was obtained by purchase, as the recent nurseries could not immediately provide the new requirements. On the other hand many nurseries soon proved to be inefficient and poorly planned, so they were soon suppressed and their number dropped to 149 on the eve of the Great War. For the numbers of seedlings distributed see: Pavari, A. (1926) *Le sistemazioni montane e i rimboschimenti*, In *L'Italia Forestale*, Florence, pp. 161-191.; e MAIC, *Relazione sull'Azienda del Demanio Forestale di Stato* cit., **207**.

[x] For an overview of the problem regarding the alpine region see P.Guichonnet, *Le popolazioni alpine fra età moderna e contemporanea*, published in Lazzarini, A. and Vendramini, F. (1991) *La montagna veneta in età contemporanea*, Rome, 1991, 11-23.

[xi] By way of example in the Alps of Lombardy and Trentino between 1871 and 1936 the population increases respectively 34% and 30%, while in the Veneto Dolomites it increased only 18%, and in Liguria one witnesses a slight contraction -1.5%. Cfr. Camaiti, A.M. (1958) *La politica montana e l'azione dell'Amministrazione Forestale*, «L'Italia Forestale e Montana», XIII, 1, 9-21. One must however note that the upward trend of the mountain population continues uninterrupted from 1861 to 1951, increases more rapidly between 1861 and 1871, and between 1911 and 1921, while between the end of 1921 and the end of the '30s there is a decrease, and finally a further recovery from 1936 to the early '50s. For an overview of the problem of demographic trends in the Italian mountains see Crestanello, E. (1993) *Il problema della montagna*, Franco Angeli, Milan.

[xii] In an article by Francesco Caldart the case of Fiumara Amusa, in the province of Reggio Calabria, is considered comparing the situation between 1910 and 1930. Caldart, F. (1930) *Sistemazioni montane, demografia e bonifica integrale*, «L'Alpe», XVII, 9, 417-423.

through the cultivation of very steep slopes and land reclamation areas[xiii]. The growth in foreign demand for agricultural goods that was recorded in this period did not make it worthwhile for landowners to introduce new technologies. They had abundant labour available at very low cost. Thus, when at the end of the 1800s American cereals took over the market, the export of agricultural products ceased. This led to a labour-intensive agriculture being operated exclusively as a social safety net for the excess workforce, even if the tendency to reduce forest areas remained intact.

Still, the industrial development recorded at the end of the 1800s resulted, directly and indirectly, in an increase in consumption of firewood and timber. Italy had no fossil fuel resources and initially the energy needs of the industry were focused on wood and charcoal, which in 1861 supplied more than 85% of the energy requirements. The use of solid and liquid fossil fuels which were entirely imported grew slowly until it reached 60% around 1910, while electricity made its timid appearance towards the end of the century, contributing only 9% to the national energy budget on the eve of the First World War. All this, coupled with the steady growth in *per capita* consumption, resulted in massive wood consumption, which, as estimated for the period, far exceeded the production capacity of the woods. In fact, the requirements had to be satisfied by the growing use of wood collected from the forest, by cutting trees and hedges and pruning crop plants, whose production increased by 50% between 1861 and 1912. The same growth was due to the need for timber for the booming construction sector[xiv]. This timber was imported from abroad in growing quantities with values increasing four-fold in the same period. After fossil fuels and cereals, imports of timber were one of the most important elements of the Italian balance of trade at the turn of the twentieth century.

The combined effect of three factors – agricultural expansion, energy requirements and production of wood – influenced the Italian woods in different ways. The expansion of agriculture and pasture triggered a rapid process of reduction in the wooded area, to which were added the effects brought about by the 1877 law. Because of this release, according to the statistics available and the comments of some experts, at least 1,000,000 hectares of

---

[xiii] The absence of technical improvements in machinery, equipment and methods of cultivation continued essencially until the beginning of the 1900s, cfr. Orlando, G. (1969), *Progressi e difficoltà dell'agricoltura* in G.Fuà, *Lo sviluppo economico in Italia. Storia dell'economia Italiana negli ultimi cento anni*, III, Milan, **20** and ff.

[xiv] Romanelli, R. (1990) *L'Italia liberale*, Bologna.

woods were eliminated. Between 1870 and 1912 there is an estimated reduction in the wooded area of 15-30%, a trend that remained unchanged at least until the end of the 1920s when it is reversed[xv]. Therefore, if it is partially true what Marsh wrote concerning the fact that Italy's 1877 forest law did not really aim at preserving existing forests, although it actually put restrictions to deforestation, it also not true that it aimed to create new ones [xvi] . As the law had little effects on preservation it also had little effects on afforestation.

Where there were no deforestation processes, temporary or definitive, one witnessed an evolution towards forms of poor silviculture. This was in terms of unit value of the stock, probably more adapted to the needs of the rural economy but preserving the resources of the woods. The most prominent example certainly refers to forms of management that in little more than 50 years led to the reversal of the relationship between coppice and standards; in 1870 coppice accounted for 40% of the wooded area and standards 60%; this relationship was reversed in 1925[xvii].

It is at this time that a profound change in the mountain landscape of the territory occurs, with a major focus on forestry where 60% of the wooded area was concentrated. Intense exploitation and multi-functioning of the woods, mainly through coppice and transformation into agricultural crops, could only intensify the already extensive hydrogeological damage, which was due to an overall reduction in wooded coverage of the slopes. Although, the practice of terracing allowed for the slowing down of water flows from the watershed. Against all these major processes affecting Italian society, the legislative measures taken were weak and the modest reforestation and hydraulic restoration interventions bear witness to this failure.

[xv] The highest value of this reduction is obtained by comparing the Castagnola statistic with data reported by Lunardoni, A. (1904), *Vini, Uve e Legnami nei trattati di commercio*, Rome, **69**. Patrone suggests instead a value equal to 15%, cfr. G.Patrone,*Cenni di geografia economica forestale,* Florence, 1970, **71**.

[xvi] Hall, cited: p 48.

[xvii] The data is obtained from the Castagnola statistics from 1870 and from the data of Carloni, P. (1926) La estensione e la distribuzione territoriale dei boschi italiani, in *L'Italia Forestale*, Florence, **44.**

Towards a new philosophy for action: the technical reflection in the early decades of the century

Together with a reduced effectiveness in quantitative terms, the implementation of reforestation and restoration interventions was problematic even from a technical point of view, leading to a reflection certainly not disconnected from the social and economic context.

Out of the discussions regarding other state organs' activity, the consortia are the main actors of the rehabilitation works of the Italian mountains up to the 1912 law. However, reports on the activities of consortia highlight a problem debated in the forestry sector for some time. It was one, which tried to explain some of the reasons for the modest effectiveness shown in achieving the objectives set. The works carried out were in fact being criticised, the consortia accused of having moved away from institutional tasks and from their original objectives, focusing on works of restoration instead of reforestation. This trend is documented in chart 1, which shows how from 1888 to 1893 there is a certain disproportion between the costs of engineering works and reforestation. A difference that is maintained in subsequent periods, with a peak in 1911-1914, summarised as 59% committed to the cost of restoration.

The criticism made to consortia and to operational choices can be interpreted briefly by reviewing the path of the Italian forestry school. At the time of its foundation in 1869 the forestry school was searching for a technical and scientific identity by looking critically at models from central European countries. From a general point of view, Germany was primarily the point of reference, even if that judgement seems to relate specifically to economic aspects, whereas the design of silvicultural methods had also benefited from the experience of the French school. Di Berenger, first director of the school of Vallombrosa, was born in Germany by French parents and had completed part of his education in Austria while still employed by the government of Vienna, before moving to Italy and the Italian forest administration.

France, at least in the period following the 1877 Forest Law[xviii], was seen as a leader in the hydrological and forestry sector. French authors had given a great impetus to this sector's scientific development thanks to their experience gained in the Alps especially with reference to the construction of weirs. In fact, Italy was not without a long tradition of studies on the subject. Bacci in 1576 had already described the need for weirs to correct the torrents of the Tiber River, an argument taken by Manni in 1618, while the construction of weirs was addressed in detail by Viviani for the Arno River in 1681. Studies continued in the following century by Frisi (1762) up to the fundamental texts of the nineteenth century by Mengotti and Bergolli when the problem was now the object of considerable public attention.

Despite this, the Italian school found itself largely unprepared to deal with hydrological and forest restoration techniques with scientific rigour. The teaching of the subjects related to this topic can be found partly in the third year of the initial courses at Vallombrosa, under the name "road and hydrological architecture in relation to the work of forests", while a course on river re-engineering would arrive later. Only with the passing of the 1888 law was there a major impetus given to reforestation within a general reorganisation of the courses. These were linked to the evolution of forest science in the international arena.

For these reasons, the debate that developed in the early 1900s focused on an assessment of the greater or lesser effectiveness of using masonry for the re-engineering of rivers with respect to reforestation. The debate does not take into account what had been said historically by Italian authors but was prompted by a reflection on the more contemporary work done so far and by the work of the French, especially Surell, Demontzey and Thiery. The French law of 1860 was based on the work of Surell, but the results of its application were not known before the 1878 Universal Exhibition in Paris where they were illustrated with drawings, photographs and scale models of the effect of the works[xix]. However, it was

---

[xviii] This is seen from the general consideration of forestry technicians and appears in A. Pavari, *Le sistemazioni montane e i rimboschimenti* cit.,**168**, 168, but also in the specific texts about this subject. Cfr. Horatiis, M.De (1930) *Istituzioni di Idronomia Montana*, Florence.

[xix] Nico, P. (1879), *Sulle condizioni forestali della Francia, relazione letta al club scientifico di Vienna il 27 Marzo 1879 dal barone A. Seckendorff, «*Nuova Rivista Forestale», II, **191**.

In the last decades of the 19th century the Italian Amministrazione Forestale began an extensive programme of photographic documentation of the reforestation and hydrological restoration works carried out throughout the peninsula documenting the work not only during the execution but often up to 15 years after their term. Many photographs were kept until a short time ago at the technologic and forestry collection of the Forestry

Demontzey's work, the technical and theoretical foundations of which appear in 1882 which had a greater influence in Italy and which caused heated debate. Giuseppe Segala reviewed the text in the *Nuova Rivista Forestale*. He recognised the merit of strongly asserting the need for good technical preparation in the construction of masonry work, which in many cases must precede or at least accompany the reforestation work: "which coming to be its complement, therefore, does not lose its great effectiveness".

The publication of Demontzey's work was of extraordinary relevance after the disastrous floods in north-eastern Italy in 1882. The analysis of the environmental disaster was traced back to large amounts of rainfall, the progressive destruction of forests, large sediment transport and lack of hydrological structures. Measures suggested to prevent the recurrence of such events are listed in a lengthy article in the *Nuova Rivista Forestale* by the engineer Alessandro Arnaud. Here there is explicit reference to the need for the construction of dams and "large" weirs, emphasizing their importance for the stability of the slopes. The need to maintain the woods is also clearly indicated but without any reference to reforestation, while the rest of the article focuses on the construction technique of the structures[xx].

It is probably for these reasons that greater attention was given to restoration works than reforestation. However, it is certainly that the beginning of the new century sees the confrontation between very conflicting opinions. In 1910, criticising a previous article by Bandi, Segala invites "young people" not to praise the woods and "exaggerate their benefits" in the prevention of landslides and floods because the causes are only partially related to the presence of woods but greatly dependent on the rainfall pattern and the amount of rain. According to the author, once some damage had occurred the only solution was to build weirs, the execution of which the Amministrazione Forestale had often been forced to do but that Bandi judged unnecessary. The article concludes by stating that it would be appropriate to have good "forest engineers" to solve all the problems of the

---

Institute of the University of Florence, but as with other materials are now missing. Agnoletti, M. (1988-1989) *Le raccolte fotografiche della Collezione Tecnologico - Forestale dell'Istituto di Selvicoltura*, Museologia Scientifica, V (3-4), 287-292.

[xx] According to the author by dam one means the work destined to reduce landslides and mudslides, while the term weir indicates the works that bar the bed of a river to limit sediment transport and reduce the force of the water. These structures were basically of three types: masonry, timber and living material. Each of these could have different features and could also be implemented in mixed marterials, eg. timber and masonry. Arnaud, A. (1884) *Briglie, Traverse e Serbatoi Artificiali*, «Nuova Rivista Forestale», VII, 134-161.

mountain economy. This stance, claiming a forestry orientation of the courses, has remained to this day.

Although Segala's criticism appears to be quite measured, reactions are vehement. In the brief analysis of the measures made by the government in the first decade of the century Sub-inspector Bandi recognises a strong negative opinion from the government on the effectiveness of the consolidation works[xxi]. In support of this position, many references to France are made, where there had been a profound re-evaluation on the work done on the restoration of mountain rivers. In the French Alps most of the expenses incurred for the many large masonry works were unnecessary, since many of them had been ruined. The blame for this failure is attributed to Demontzey, the main supporter of the need for these structures and whose work had significantly deviated from the work of Surell. In 1841, Surell suggested a rather sober use of these interventions, considered as exceptions and not the rule, denouncing the flaws[xxii].

In truth, Surell's definition had been negatively judged by Lechalas who in his introduction to Thiery's "Restauration des montagnes" criticises Surrell's interpretation of the torrential phenomena[xxiii]. It is important to note that Demontzey had changed his mind about his initial conviction, stating in an 1896 work considered his "technical testament" that the most effective action could only be performed by large forests and that one should abandon the philosophy of intensive construction works in favour of the reforestation of large areas.

[xxi] The tone of the article is quite strong and they talk about "fighting the insane undertaking of the works of protection," stating that "twenty years onwards the weirs will be a myth". The author responds point by point to the observations of Segala denying that landslides and floods could happen in watersheds covered with woods. Cfr. Bandi, V. (1910), *La sistemazione dei bacini montani ovvero parere e non essere*, «L'Alpe», no. 6-7, 161-171.

[xxii] It is worth mentioning some of Surell's text about the weirs: "Le traverse o serre sono il genere di difesa più efficace quando si tratti di proteggere una limitata striscia di proprietà rivierasche......il loro effetto si ridurrebbe in un certo modo a rialzare il letto parallelamente a se stesso di una quantità pari alla loro altezza...per attenuare tanto quanto è possibile questo difetto, bisognerebbe dare ai muri una grande altezza fuori letto, ma allora le cascate dell'acqua diventano formidabili e gli scavi da esse prodotti rovinosi. L'impiego infine di un siffatto genere di sbarramento intrapreso su larga scala potrebbe riuscire pericoloso, determinando, nel caso in cui uno o più di codesti muri venissero squarciati da una piena, dei veri disastri." Cfr. Surell, A. (1842), *Etudes sur les torrents des Hautes Alpes*, Paris. ["The weirs or serre are the type of protection that is more effective when one wants to protect a limited strip of riverine property ......their effect is reduced in a certain way to raising the river bed by a height equal to the river height ...to mitigate this fault as much as you can one should give the walls a great height out of the bed but then the water turns into formidable waterfalls and the holes they produce are disastrous. The use then of such a kind of barrier on a large scale could become dangerous, resulting in true disasters in case one or more of these walls were pierced by flooding"].

[xxiii] Thiery, E. (1891), *Restauration des montagnes*, Paris, 1-17.

However, the controversy between the two forest inspectors does not go unnoticed, because immediately in the following issue of the *Alpe* a further article appears from inspector Canciani. He was employed on specific mountain restoration works and seeks to distance himself from the controversial tone taken by the discussion. He considers the two types of intervention as equally important but still believes in mandatory reforestation and useful engineering works to be made only where they are needed, calling for more flexibility in the choice of method.

A few years later in an article, Di Tella reinforced the analysis of the first French experience and its negative influence at a national level. In criticising the setting that seemed to favour construction work compared to reforestation he observes that initially the legislator was able to correctly identify the second element that had to have absolute prevalence. In fact, the work of the forest consortia initially gave priority to this aspect. With the publication of Demontzey's first work, and because of the visit to the French Alps made by students of the Vallombrosa School along with representatives from the Ministry of Agriculture, there was instead a turnaround that led to favouring construction work.

The opinion of Di Tella was undoubtedly influential. Not only was he the leader of the course on "Torrent Correction" at Istituto Forestale di Vallombrosa [Royal Forestry Institute of Vallombrosa], but he was also the author of the famous pamphlet "The woods against the torrent". This was published in 1912 by the Italian Touring Club's advertising board for woods and pasture to indicate the urgency of reforestation and the restoration of mountain watersheds. Both in this informative text and in the handouts of the lectures held at Vallombrosa he states, "the woods are the means for consolidation and more effective protection of soil exposed to the fury of meteoric erosion". However, cases where the construction of weirs appears necessary are clearly contemplated and there is therefore a denial of the need for forestation works.

The caution expressed on the effectiveness of weirs was undoubtedly the result of an assessment of the frequent failures to which the use of these structures had been subject in Italy. Di Tella also notes that the opinion on the work of the school of Demontzey must necessarily take into account other aspects of the social and economic environment of the mountains. The preference given to weirs in France was also linked to the open hostility of mountain people against the reforestation undertaken under the 1860 law, a problem that also goes with all reforestations and forest law enforcement in Italy[xxiv]. It was thought possible therefore to solve the problem more quickly with expensive but quick works rather than longer term with a waiting period before beneficial effects of reforestation occur. This distinction was poorly recognised by the mountain communities. It is why the intensification of measures in favour of reforestation and *vincoli* of any kind developed into open hostility towards foresters and the woods. This was a feature, which occurred over a long period as is readily observed by the number of penalties imposed on offenders[xxv]. Such reactions paved the way for rethinking the policy for the mountains that, although there was a need to reduce human pressure, it was also necessary to promote sustainable social and economic development and not merely the imposition of *vincoli*. If in fact there are publications that enhance the positive effect of reforestation in the restoration of some mountain watersheds, used as examples to demonstrate the ineffectiveness of the major construction works, they also highlight the effectiveness of simple grazing bans to limit hydrogeological disruption.

Beyond the purely technical opinions, one can catch a glimpse of other reasons that influenced the positions taken in this matter. From the government's point of view, the opinion expressed by the Minister of Agriculture, Raineri, can be seen in two ways. During the discussion of the bill to establish the forest domain, the Minister expressed scepticism about the construction works for retaining walls and declared that one should focus more on reforestation. It may be in fact that this judgement is not incompatible with reasons linked to expenditure rather than technical reasons, given the cost of the large masonry work and increased references to the use of systems such as living fences and fascine bundles or small dry stone walls made from materials found on site[xxvi]. A view supported by the actions of other MPs, who also criticise the excessive cost of the *per diem* for the

---

[xxiv] A. Pavari, *Le sistemazioni montane e i rimboschiment* cit., **161-191**. The average of anual fines for violations of the *vincolo* was 17,209 in the five years from 1901-905, 28,379 in 1911 and was later reduced to 23,197 in the period 1914-24. Cfr. Jandolo, E., (1929), *La montagna e le leggi per la bonifica integrale*, «L'Alpe», no. 1, pp. 5-13. Things did not go better in the following period given that the activity of the Milizia Forestale [Forest Militia] agreed to increase 30,000 forest fines in 1925 which went up to 48,000 in 1928. Cfr. (1929),*Il problema montano e forestale al parlamento*, «L'Alpe», no. 8, **347**.

[xxv] The average of annual fines for violations of the *vincolo* was of 17,209 in the five years from 1901-905, 28,379 in 1911 and was later reduced to 23,197 in the period of 1914-24. Cfr. Jandolo, E. *La montagna e le leggi per la bonifica integrale* cit. p.7. Things will not go better in the following period given that the activity of the Milizia Forestale agreed to raise 30,000 forest fines in 1925, which went up to 48,000 in 1928. Cfr. (1929), *Il problema montano e forestale al parlamento*, «L'Alpe», no. 8, **347**.

[xxvi] This is the content of the intervention of engineer Carlo Valentini at the congress on forests of 1909. (1910), *Gli Atti del Congresso Forestale Italiano di Bologna* , «L'Alpe», no. 10-11, **313**.

work of engineers in Italy[xxvii]. However, that introduces a further element to evaluate the controversy in place, if one reflects on the technical profiles involved in the discussion.

Not coincidentally, Maganzini, chairman of the Technical Committee for the works on the watershed of the Sele River, was in fact in favour of consolidation works and criticised the effectiveness of the 1877 and 1888 laws. He notes that considering reforestation exclusively was the cause of the antipathy against, and failure of, the laws. He suggested that one needed to associate forestry with engineering as was the case in France, Germany, Switzerland, Austria, and other "civilised" countries. Maganzini's words are not surprising, given that the article reproduced the press conference text read at the headquarters of the Italian Engineering Society in Rome on April 19, 1911. Considering that the year before, Perona, director of the Istituto di Vallombrosa, had also come out strongly against construction work one may think that probably there was a conflict of jurisdiction, if not a conflict between foresters and engineers to ensure they had the contracts to execute the works[xxviii]. But for the fact that most of the restoration works were made by the Genio Civile [civil engineering state body] with funds from the Ministry of Agriculture rather than from the Ministry of Public Works[xxix]. The role of engineers was still relevant in the Scuola Forestale [Forestry School] as the course was specifically dedicated to forest hydrological restorations. With the proposed new system of studies approved after moving the institute to Florence in 1914, the course was led by Manfredi de Horatiis who graduated from the school of Vallombrosa, but also had an honours degree in civil engineering from the University of Palermo.

Observations on an existing imbalance between engineering and reforestation works are repeated until the end of the 1930s when Di Tella publishes an article with the same title as the one published 16 years before and with almost the same content, renewing his call for a different line of action. However, an evolution is noted in the concept of restoration even

---

[xxvii] According to the Hon. Masi "sono più le diarie che prendono gli ingegneri per andare sul luogo che non il valore del lavoro stesso". Bandi., cit., **166** ["it is the daily allowances that make engineers go to the place more than the value of the work itself"]

[xxviii] This problem deserves some reflection given its actuality. That is indirectly confirmed by Di Tella's article in 1934: Tella, G. Di (1934), *Per la montagna italiana - Dalla legge forestale del 20 giugno 1877 alla legge sulla bonifica integrale del 13 febbraio 1933* –XI, «L'Alpe», no. 1, 1-3.
We are however in a difficult period for the Istituto Forestale [Institute of Forests] which had been moved to Florence thanks to the 1912 law, also to compensate for a sharp decline in subscribers. Cfr. S. Muzzi, *Vicende storiche della scuola forestale italiana*, in L'Italia Forestale nel Centenario….cit., **370-391**.

[xxix] Carullo, F. (1915) *Politica forestale e tecnica delle sistemazioni idrauliche*, «L'Italia Forestale e Montana», V, no. 3, **94**.

from an engineering point of view, which seeks to overcome the drawbacks, which previously occurred. Initially there were in fact interventions focused mainly on rivers, while later the proposal is to intervene instead on the whole water catchment to influence the water regime by decreasing the flow of the tributaries. As early as 1916, the creation of large basins in morphologically suitable areas to collect water and trap alluvial materials by stopping them from being deposited in large dams was suggested. Besides regulating floods, large basins could be used to produce electricity, then strongly emerging, thus providing a further service. A few years later a new concept was also introduced, stating that it was not always necessary to build high dams but one could use areas of floodplain to let the waters expand, trap solid materials and slow down their flow, thus referring to the modern notion of "expansion box".

It was not, however, in weir construction techniques that innovative concepts could be developed in Italy compared to other European countries but rather in true reforestation techniques where it offered a significant contribution. The poor characteristics of the soils, the climate with distinct features of drought-prone reforestation areas and the steepness of mountain slopes forced not only the identification of species adapted to these conditions but also the development of specific implementation techniques which also assumed a certain importance across the rest of the Mediterranean area. It is worth mentioning the terracing needed to collect the little remaining soil and prevent the runoff of water, which was very expensive in terms of labour, often forced to make a profit by chipping away at the rock with a pick. A special mention must be made of the Allegretti method developed in Sardinia in 1919 in very difficult conditions. This soon became the most effective method for hot arid climates. These years were crucial because they developed expertise that made it possible from a technical point of view to expand large reforestation programmes in the following decades. Once again, the conditions of Italy, very different from those of the countries of Central Europe, forced the development of specific techniques that could not use proven solutions in very different geological and climatic conditions. This issue has strong continuity in the history of Italian and Mediterranean silviculture and forestry management in comparison to the Nordic countries.

The new philosophy of State intervention and the organic vision of the mountain problem

The establishment of the State domain in 1910 overturned the philosophy of non-intervention followed previously, setting out the increased capacity of the State to pursue public interest. The action of the government should substantially encourage private owners, but in cases where there were protected forests and reforestation of mountain watersheds and private owners were unable to intervene, the State had the duty to replace them to protect public interest. This was the beginning of the Luzzatti law shared by other economists of that period[xxx]. The first decades of the public company's activities aimed particularly at creating state forests and defining their management. They are characterised by a significant increase recorded from the financial statements but the costs of reforestation appear rather limited. However, the further important legislative measure in favour of reforestation and restoration works was the law of December 30, 1923, no. 3267. The law is also known as Serpieri law, named after the then Secretary of State, the major architect of this project. It was supposed to represent the basic structure of the legal system for the Italian forests, upon which all its subsequent development would be based. The principle, that in damaged mountain watersheds it is first necessary to intervene with hydrological and forest restoration works, was stated, integrating it with agricultural and land improvement restoration works referring to the "organic" character of the measure in comparison to previous measures.

In title (chapter/section) II of the legislation, the material was divided into hydrological and forest restoration of mountain watersheds and reforestation to consolidate land with *vincoli (obligations)*. In the first part it was established that the works were going to be carried out at the expense of the State, especially reforestation, consolidation and connected building works which would be the responsibility of the Ministry of Agriculture and Forests, while hydrological works were immediately considered to be the responsibility of the Ministry of Public Works. In the second part, the law ordered that both the Amministrazione Forestale

[xxx] Bolla, G.G. (1919) *Gli scritti di politica e legislazione forestale di Luigi Luzzatti,* in «Annali dell'Accademia dei Georgofili», 97, p.3. The validity of this initiative was also underlined in the post-war period by Einaudi, who opposed the usefulness of the forestry domain to the harmfulness of the fiscal domain, able of more effectively pursueing public interest. Einaudi, L. (1848), *Principi di scienza della finanza*, Boringhieri, Turin, **1**.

and the provinces and communes could, individually or organised in consortia, promote the reforestation of land with *vincoli.*

The imposition of the hydrogeological requirement brought about by this measure extended across all types of land, which because of its forms of exploitation could be denuded by public damage, lose stability or disturb the water regime. This measure extended the land with *vincoli* to approximately 7,000,000 hectares compared to 3,825,548 estimated in 1879. In addition to these initiatives, the public company of the State Forests Domain was reorganised specifically in order to allow for the formation of timber reserves, given the strategic role of this resource and the increasing dependence on imports. The management of municipal and other woods would be subject to economic plans.

The 1923 law not only rearranged and confirmed the 51 legislative measures operating in the kingdom, to which 27 measures of Austrian origin were added and linked to the new provinces, but regarded the forest policy as an element of a broader economic and hydrological policy. This was the intention even if later objections were made that in fact the truly economic aspects were almost ignored. The mountain regions were therefore considered as a whole, with the thinking not only of imposing *vincoli* but of making general progress in the mountain economy across all its sectors. The approach was considered an indispensable condition to ensure the protection of the woods and the control of erosion. This philosophy was heavily influenced by resolution no. 3256 of December 1923 on hydrological reclamation. This resolution affirmed with greater force than previously the concept of unity of river watersheds by stating that a single guideline does not define an organic restoration. This was followed by the law of May 18, 1924, no. 753 on transformation of lands of public interest. In 1929, these two laws were associated with the common denomination of whole land reclamation, to which fascism gave a lot of emphasis[xxxi]. However, for a measure that formulated this concept organically one had to

[xxxi] Jandolo, E. (1919) *La montagna e le leggi per la bonifica integrale,* «l'Alpe», no. 1, pp. 5-13. The same article was preceded by an introduction in which he remembered the "memorable"words of Arnaldo Mussolini on the people of Itally on October 4, 1929: "...che la bonifica integrale deve essere non solo quella delle pianure malariche, ma anche quella delle colline e delle montagne in un tutto armonico e inscindibile; che il problema forestale non si risolve se non considerandolo come un elemento del più vasto e complesso problema della bonifica del monte". ["...that the reclamation must be not only that of the malarial lowlands but also that of the hills and of the moutains into a harmonious and indivisible wholeness; and that the problem of the forests is not solved if one does not consider it as an element of the broader and more complex problem of restoring the mountain".]

wait for the R.D. of February 13, 1933 on whole land reclamation[xxxii]. The unified vision of the problem and the aim of reducing the problem of skills created further hopes, making one even speak of "battle won" and of the culmination of decades of effort around this issue[xxxiii]. The vision was perhaps appropriate to the crowning of a legislative effort, but very optimistic when compared to practical results.

Some quantitative assessments on interventions

Despite the character of the organic measures mentioned, the work of reforestation was still producing modest results. This is not surprising when one notes that between 1870 and 1938 only 7% of the financial resources were assigned to reforestation and restoration, while 93% of the funds went to land reclamation works on the plains. The analysis of the practical effects of the measures, more than anything else, gives an idea of the results achieved; it is worth remembering that in approximately 80 years only 194,720 hectares were reforested. It is however useful to point out the responsibilities of the various agencies involved and some aspects of the temporal and spatial scales of the interventions.

From the foregoing one can clearly identify several key bodies – the Reforestation Consortia, the Amministrazione Forestale known as the Ministry of Agriculture, Industry and Commerce, and the public company for State Forests Domains – engaged in the financing and implementation of reforestation and restoration works. The intervention of these individual bodies in terms of expenditure was not equal, and the amount spent also varied from one region to another. In addition, a small part of this work was carried out with funds from the Ministry of Public Works. Although it would take too long to analyse the quantitative data in detail, these are widely discussed in a long article by Generoso Patrone[xxxiv], it is useful to make a few brief references before developing the case further in this present paper.

[xxxii] For a broad overview of the models of action of the law see the volume by Serpieri, A. (1931), *La legge sulla bonifica integrale nel primo anno di applicazione*, M.A.F., Rome.
[xxxiii] Tella, G. Di (1934), *Per la montagna italiana* , cit. **1-3**.
[xxxiv] Patrone analyses in his long article all results considering geographic regions, administrative regions and individual provinces, proposing to subdivide the period considered into the following periods: 1867-1914, 1914-24, 1924-33, 1933-40, 1940-46, 1946-50. The data was extrapolated from its publication to which we refer for detailed analysis. Patrone, G. (1952), *Il contributo dello Stato e degli Enti alle sistemazioni montane e al miglioramento e all'ampliamento dei boschi e dei pascoli dal 1867 al 1950*, L'Italia forestale e montana, 321-349.

In terms of expenditure, across Italy and throughout the period analysed the Amministrazione Forestale contributed 73%, the Consortia 21% and the Public Company 6%. Expenses supported by the reforestation consortia range from the highest in the Alps at 33% and none in Sardinia, showing a gradual reduction from the northern Apennines (26%), the central Apennines (20%), 13% to Sicilia and 5% to the southern Apennines. On the contrary, the amounts invested by the Amministrazione Forestale/the Forest Administration decrease from the southern Apennines (90%) to the Alps (63%).

One can clearly see differences in the results achieved in the first 60 years of state intervention, i.e. until the land reclamation law, when compared with the subsequent period. In the period between 1867 and 1914, one observes the prevalence of the intervention of the Forestry Consortia at 65% of total expenditure, followed by the Amministrazione Forestale [Forestry Administration] at 30%, and the Public Company at 5%. In the subsequent period, i.e. 1914-1924, the intervention of the Amministrazione Forestale increases to 74%, while the expenditure of the Public Company is at 8% and the Consortia 18%.

The trend remains constant even in subsequent periods, such as from 1924 to 1950. Government intervention remains around 80%, with a reduced percentage achieved by the Public Company and an ever-decreasing intervention by the consortia that is down to 4% by 1950. The figures confirm the facts of a change in policy in this sector from 1910 onwards, which is increasingly becoming a decisive initiative of the State.

From a geographical perspective the Alps as a whole account for 32% of the resources involved across the period considered, the northern Apennines for 13%, the central Apennines for 20%, the southern Apennines for 16%, Sicilia 14% and Sardinia for 5%[xxxv]. For a more accurate evaluation of these parameters one must, however, keep in mind the varying extents of the individual mountain regions which is greatest in the Alps, followed by the central, the southern and the northern Apennines respectively, and also the different conditions of hydrogeological damage. In general, the cost per hectare decreases from the islands to the Mezzogiorno and the Alps. Patrone explains this being due to the most degraded condition being in the southern regions. Appearing significant in this context are

---

[xxxv] The subdivision adopted by Patrone considers Liguria and Emilia-Romagna as being part of the northern Apennines; Tuscany, Marche, Umbria, Lazio and Abruzzo-Molise as part of the central Apennines; Campania, Puglia, Basilicata and Calabria as being part of the southern Apennines. Ibidem, **334**.

the very high costs per hectare for Sicily, about three times those of the Alps and the southern and central Apennines; in contrast, the total expenditure is greater in the Alps, with an amount double or, at least, much higher than for the other regions.

The pattern of interventions in different regions varies, for example in the first period of 47 years no interventions took place in Lazio. However, interventions are greatly represented in the Alpine regions (Veneto 13.7%, Lombardia 12.2%, Piemonte 10.4%) due to the better conditions in which the consortia could operate. This was due in part to the decreased conflicts with local populations about the limitations posed by reforestation on grazing. Some provinces attracted important shares of the money spent in the regional context. In Piemonte 68% of interventions were made in the province of Cuneo, where in the watershed of the Prebec River some impressive weirs were built in stone, later destroyed by the floods that started the debate about the effectiveness of such actions. The same happened in Calabria and in Cosenza (60%) and in Campania with Napoli (65%).

Turning to the actual reforested areas in the period 1861-1950 only 194,720 hectares were reforested, with an average of 2,346 hectares per year. 26.9% of new forests were created in the Alps, 15% in the northern Apennines, 25.7% in the central Apennines, 19.9% in the southern Apennines, 5.7% in Sicilia and 6.8% in Sardinia. This indicates an increase in forested area more than proportional to the forest already present in southern Italy and less than proportional in northern Italy. The result is justified by the need for a greater effort in areas where denuded surfaces were far more extensive.

An interesting observation is that the Amministrazione Forestale probably paid less attention than either the Consortia or the Public Company to reforestation compared to hydrological restorations. In fact, looking at the expenditure of the three entities and the land reforested by each one there is a lower proportion of reforestation due to the Amministrazione, which could suggest that a certain proportion of the cost was transferred to restoration works rather than reforestation. On the other hand, as already stated earlier, most of the works were made by the Genio Civile with funds from the Ministry of Agriculture. The positive role of the new laws enacted in the early decades of the twentieth century is clear, however, as confirmed by the growth rate of the wooded area. This is at a minimum (800 hectares per year) during the period 1867-14 and higher in 1933-1940 with 8,191 hectares. By increasing some of the expenditure the reforestation body grows, however, to a lesser extent overall, which again means that restoration prevails over reforestation.

As already seen by the expenditure, from 1867 to 1914 the consortia are the ones that reforest, while after 1914 it is the Amministrazione Forestale that always takes a more active role. From 1867 to 1950 the expansion of the wooded area is guaranteed as 57% by the Amministrazione Forestale, as 18% by the Public Company and as 25% by the Consortia. The contribution of the three entities is different between the geographic regions, for example in the southern Apennines the Amministrazione accounts for 83% but only for 43% in the northern Apennines. The Public Company intervenes significantly in Sardinia (47%) and very little in Sicily (6%), while the Consortia have done most in the northern Apennines and in the Alps at 41% and 39%, but were minimally involved in Sardinia (0.4%) and in the southern Apennines (4%).

It is interesting to evaluate the action of reforestation through some important case studies. One example is that of the work on the watershed of the Sele River in Campania which was carried out at the beginning of the 1900s for the protection of the future Puglia Aqueduct, the costs of which were paid entirely by the State. The study carried out by a committee of experts established in 1901 included the technical specifications set out in the law of June 26, 1902 and the R.D. of January 1, 1903. Here the municipalities involved in the project (located in the provinces of Avellino and Salerno) were identified and the technical provisions for interventions were stated. The manuscript account of the work carried out in 1910 confirms the negative judgement of the effects of the Forest Acts of 1877 and the decisive action of fire (used to extend pastures), with the consequent development of erosion phenomena.

The watershed area consisted of 826 ha of denuded land, 563 ha of woods with *vincoli*, 140 ha of woods with no *vincoli* and 755 ha of land with no *vincoli* and arable crops. The works carried out were for correction (using masonry, both dry and mixed) to modify and improve the slope and the river beds, and works of reforestation to stop landslides. The intention was thus to stop the degradation of the banks, provide absorbency for rainwater and moderate it's effects, even if the actions were sometimes not sufficient to achieve the results through suppressing pasture and building weirs, docks, living fences and fascine bundles. Trees were planted, mostly black pine, Corsican pine and Scots pine, with reforestation either by sowing or digging holes. The prominent role of these species was confirmed as early as 1893 with their presence in all the major Italian forest nurseries and through the information on intercropping, a method better suited to the south of Italy. The report notes that at the end of 1910 there were still 920 hectares to be reforested but that there were significant problems due to the refusal of the municipalities to restrict grazing areas and in such cases seedlings were often protected from cattle with wire fences. Table 1 shows the breakdown of expenditure in the period under consideration and that in fact the costs of restoration works are not prevalent, a point which indirectly favours the views expressed at the time by Maganzini as chairman of the Technical Committee.

Table 1: Statement of expenses incurred for reforestation and restoration work on the watershed of the Sele River from 1903 to 1910.

		Expenses (lire)		
Year	**Reforestation in Hectares**	**Reforestation**	**Engineering works**	**Other expenses**
1903	11	3274	1244	
1904	52	9970	17498	
1905	53	11031	7490	
1906	59	6908	8000	
1907	42	8649		
1908	80	11001		
1909	107	11776	350	
1910	110	16496		
Total	**515**	**79140**	**34585**	**21413**

Both here and in other interventions in the Mezzogiorno one observes a wide use of living fences and pickets built with plant material. In the case of the work on the Bagni River in the Catanzaro province the costs related to works done with timber amount to more than 50% of the total, while the reforestation work absorbed only 18% of the costs. In this area

8 km of living fences were also planted, which together with those with timber are now being rediscovered by environmental engineering.

The trend reversal and the achievement of the objectives: concluding remarks

The decade following the end of the Second World War finally marked a real turnaround, which was not only realized through legislative measures but rather through the profound changes in social and economic conditions. It was undoubtedly the legislative measures which were effective in 1949 and 1950 regarding construction work sites and reforestation, under the Cassa per il Mezzogiorno, and on the extraordinary interventions within the low-lying areas of the centre north, but above all it was the law of July 25, 1952 initially proposed by Fanfani. The main purpose of the measures was not so much to create new forests but rather that they had a social purpose, and in fact especially in the centre-south hundreds of reforestation yards were created which had the merit of reducing unemployment. However, once the mountain regions were released from human pressure because of the developments that decreased the labour force in agriculture coupled with the technological progress in that sector, the destinies of the woods and mountain areas were disconnected from the growth in the national population.

This triggered a process that in fifty years would lead to the reforestation of approximately 800,000 hectares and the achievement of the objectives defined more than a century earlier[xxxvi]. Added to which was a general growth in the woods that would lead them to increase in area by almost 40% when compared to the 1800s[xxxvii]. Even the drive to increase the extent of coniferous forests, compared to a drive towards deciduous, which was aimed at coping with the chronic shortage of timber, had achieved a rise in the formation of these forests from 15% in 1870 to about 60%. This was at the expense of the broadleaf trees. These results come at a very different historic moment for mountain areas, affected now by a process of reduction of population and natural afforestation of

[xxxvi] Even in 1926 it was stated that an area of woods equivalent to 7,250,000 ha would have been sufficient to cover the needs of national timber; now the woods are calculated in over 8,000,000 hectares and cover only a small part of those needs. Cfr. Merendi, A. (1926), *Politica forestale e realtà*, «L'Alpe», XIII, no.8, **245**.

[xxxvii] The uncertainty about the real extent of the increase of the woods in Italy is due to different detection criteria, a problem related not only to the 19th century statistics but also to the existing National Forestry Inventory data, of 1985 and ISTAT which differ substantially about what is meant by wooded surface. Some values may indicate an increase even hire than reported here that is still reliable for a rough estimate.

abandoned land. And also at a time when, in an international timber market, Italy is now a processing country which buys almost all wood from abroad. The calls made in 1961, at the national congress on reforestation for the need to extend Italian forests to meet the needs of timber appear therefore misleading. On closer inspection, there was no economic planning for reforestation; one used what was available in nurseries not thinking about the economic results with regard to a possible timber market. In addition to this, economic conditions that were taking place in mountain forest exploitation and the lack of high economic value forests would always penalise domestic production when compared to foreign timber[xxxviii].

The new reforestations probably contributed to the improvement of the hydrogeological conditions of the mountain but the lack of silvicultural treatments in totally artificial formations produced stands often of poor quality and had no impact on timber production. These were characterised by excessive high density, mechanical instability and various diseases[xxxix]. The functions of land improvement performed by conifers relating to soil quality and their role as preparation species for a subsequent introduction of broadleaf trees was not been followed by the establishment of new woods. These formations now represent a rather stable phase of the landscape. It was thus identified, even if belatedly, as a "landscape of the state", which in a certain sense was an attempt to impose a view of the state administration, as opposed to a "social landscape" created by shepherds and farmers. A situation not too different from the present time , where afforestation is promoted and financed by the European Union, both in terms of re-naturalisation and artificial forestation[xl]. While at the beginning of the last century there were only about 4.000.000ha of forests, today in Italy there are 10.500.000 and afforestation policies make even less sense than sixty year ago.

[xxxviii] This problem explicitly requires the introduction by Camaiti, A. (1961), *La politica dei rimboschimenti e della ricostituzione dei boschi degradati*, in *Atti del congresso nazionale sui rimboschimenti e la ricostituzione dei boschi degradati*, Accademia Italiana di Scienze Forestali, Florence, 1-10.

[xxxix] For a typical case of reforestation in a former agricultural area see: Agnoletti, M., Mercurio, R. (1996), *Rimboschimenti in terreni ex agricoli: il caso della fattoria di Gargonza,* Accademia Petrarca di Lettere Arti e Scienze, Atti e Memorie, vol. LVII, 341-361.

[xl] For the impact of the increase of forests on the rural landscape see: M.Agnoletti, ed. (2012). *Italian Historical Rural Landscapes. Cultural values for the environment and rural development*, Springer Verlag, Dordrecht.

Figure 1: Expenses incurred by the consortia for restoration and reforestation work from 1888 to 1914.

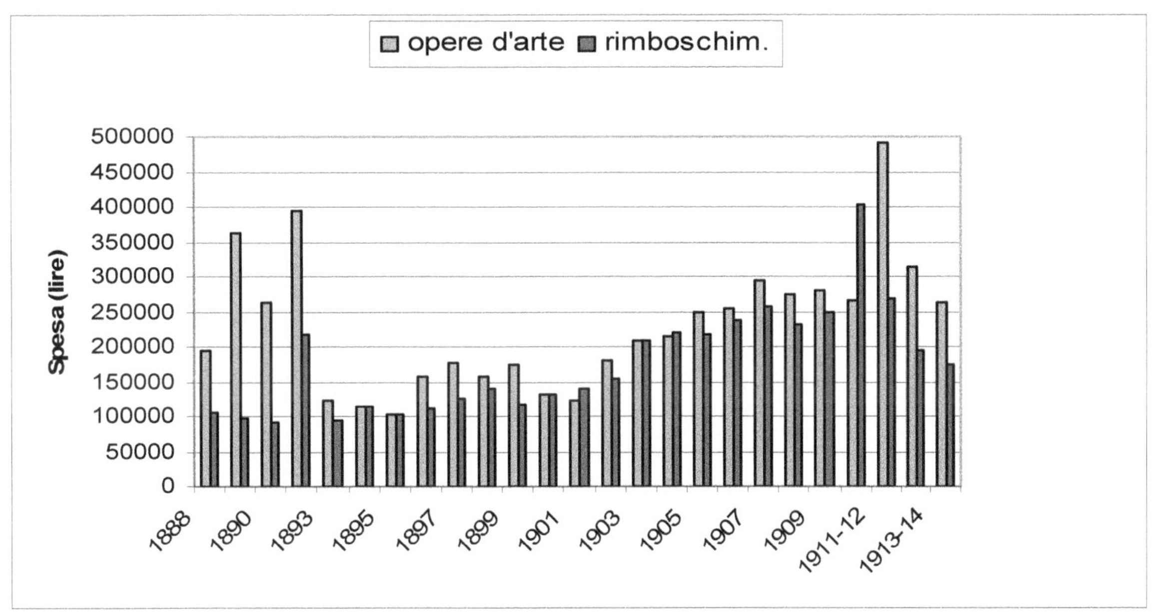

[Blue (first) bars: engineering works; brown (second) bars: reforestation works]

Figure 2: Expenses incurred for reforestation and hydrological restorations by the Ministry of Agriculture (MAIC), by the Public Company of the State Forests Domain, and by reforestation consortia (millions of lire in 1952 – data processed from the work of Patrone).

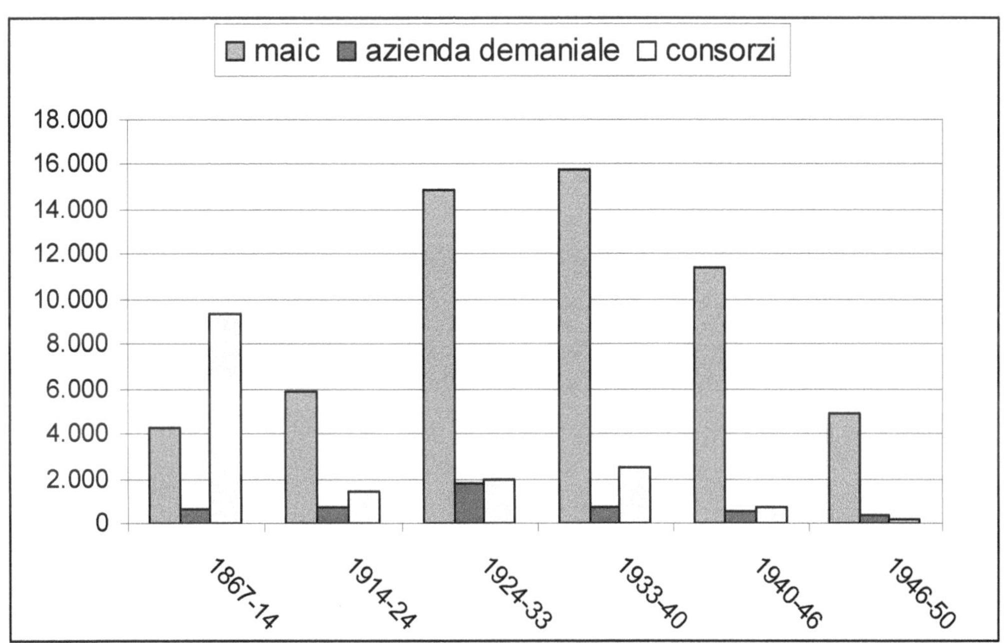

[Blue (first) bars: Ministry of Agriculture; brown (second) bars: Public Company of the State Forests Domain; yellow (third) bars: Consortia]

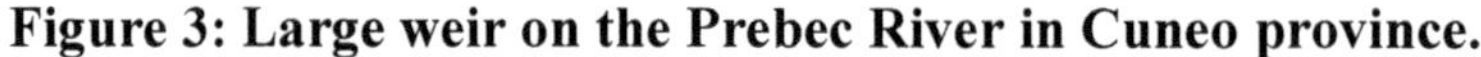

Figure 3: Large weir on the Prebec River in Cuneo province.

Figure 4: Wooded living fence. Burrone Pomice, Naples province.

Figure 5: Construction of a retaining wall in the municipality of Poppi, Arezzo province.

Figure 6: Forestry nursery of Castelluccio, Bagni di Porretta (BO).

References

Agnoletti, M. (1988-1989) *Le raccolte fotografiche della Collezione Tecnologico - Forestale dell'Istituto di Selvicoltura*, Museologia Scientifica, **V** (3-4), 287-292.

Agnoletti, M. (1996) Mercurio R., *Rimboschimenti in terreni ex agricoli: il caso della fattoria di Gargonza,* Accademia Petrarca di Lettere Arti e Scienze, Atti e Memorie, **vol. LVII**, pp. 341-361.

Agnoletti, M. (1999) *Foreste e industria del legno dall'Unità d'Italia al ventennio fascista,* in: SEHA-Departamento de historia e instituciones economicas UPV/EHU, IX Congress of Agrarian History, Zarautz, 707-720.

Agnoletti, M. (2001) *Fra storia e tecnica. Sviluppi e tendenze della storia forestale*, in *Storia e Risorse Forestali,* published by M. Agnoletti supplement to volume XLVIII of the Annali dell'Accademia Italiana di Scienze Forestali, Florence, 1-35.

Andreocci, A.(1932) *Criteri di sistemazione montana*, «L'Alpe», **no. 2-3**, 52-56.

Armiero, M., (2011) *A rugged nation, Mountains and the Making of Modern Italy*. Cambridge: The White Horse Press.

Arnaud, A. (1884) *Briglie, Traverse e Serbatoi Artificiali*, «Nuova Rivista Forestale», **VII**, 134-161.

(1959) *Azienda di Stato per le Foreste Demaniali*, Soc. A.B.E.T.E., Rome.

Bacci, A. (1576) *Del Tevere lib. 3. All'Ill.mo Senato e Popolo Romano*, Venice.

Bandi, V. (1910) *La sistemazione dei bacini montani ovvero parere e non essere*, «L'Alpe», **no. 6-7**, 161-171.

Bardini, C. (1991) *L'economia energetica italiana (1863-1913): una prospettiva inconsueta per lo studio del processo di industrializzazione*, «Rivista di storia economica», **8**, 81-114.

Bergolli, G. (1847) *Delle serre o chiuse nei torrenti fiumi*, Modena.

Bolla, G. G. (1919) *Gli scritti di politica e legislazione forestale di Luigi Luzzatti,* in «Annali dell'Accademia dei Georgofili», **97**.

Borghesani, G. (1909) *Le origini della questione forestale in Italia e l'opera del Marchese Luigi Tanari, senatore del Regno*, «L'Alpe», **4**, 97-111.

Caldart, F.(1930) *Sistemazioni montane, demografia e bonifica integrale*, «L'Alpe», **XVII**, 9, 417-423.

Camaiti, A. M. (1958) *La politica montana e l'azione dell'Amministrazione Forestale*, «L'Italia Forestale e Montana», **XIII**, 1, 9-21.

Camaiti, A. (1961) *La politica dei rimboschimenti e della ricostituzione dei boschi degradati*, in *Atti del congresso nazionale sui rimboschimenti e la ricostituzione dei boschi degradati*, Accademia Italiana di Scienze Forestali, Florence, 1-10.

Canciani, G. (1910) *La sistemazione dei bacini montani*, «L'Alpe», **8-9**, 229-233.

Cappuccini, G. (1928) *Come e perché si sistemano i bacini montani*, «L'Alpe», **6**, 157-165.

Carloni, P. (1926) La estensione e la distribuzione territoriale dei boschi italiani, in *L'Italia Forestale*, Florence.

Carullo, F. (1950), *Politica forestale e tecnica delle sistemazioni idrauliche*, «L'Italia Forestale e Montana», **V**, 3.

Carullo, F. (1951) *La sistemazione idraulico-forestale dei bacini montani e leggi 10 Agosto 1950, n 646 e 647*, «L'Italia Forestale e Montana», **5**, 217-231.

Caruso, C. (1977) *Evoluzione della legislazione forestale nazionale in materia di rimboschimenti,*« L'Italia Forestale e Montana», **XXXII**, 4, 141-146.

Corpo Reale Forestale, Ripartimento di Avellino, *Compendio delle relazioni sui lavori di sistemazione forestale e rimboschimento eseguiti nell'Alto Bacino del Sele dal 1903 al 1910.* Handwritten, Dipartimento di Scienze e Tecnologie Ambientali Forestali, University of Florence

Corpo Reale Forestale, Ripartimento di Catanzaro, *Relazione sui rimboschimenti e sui lavori di sistemazione di torrenti e consolidamento di frane e burroni eseguiti nel dipartimento forestale di Catanzaro a tutto il 31 Dicembre 1910.* Typed, Dipartimento di Scienze e Tecnologie Ambientali Forestali, University of Florence.

Crestanello, E. (1993) *Il problema della montagna*, Franco Angeli, Milan.

De Horatiis, M. (1930) *Istituzioni di Idronomia Montana*, Florence.

Demontzey, P. (1882) *Traité pratique du reboisement et du gazonnement des montagnes*, Paris.

Demontzey, P. (1896) *Le retenues d'eau et le reboisement dans le bassin de la Durance*, Aix.

Einaudi, L. (1948) *Principi di scienza della finanza*, Boringhieri, Turin.

Frisi, P. (1762) *Del modo di regolare i fiumi e i torrenti*, Lucca.

Guichonnet, P. (1991) *Le popolazioni alpine fra età moderna e contemporanea*, published in A. Hall, M., Earth Repair. A transatlantic History of Environmental Restoration, University of Virginia

Herzen, A. (1889) *Rimboscamenti e inondazioni, «*Nuova Rivista Forestale», 101-118.

Jandolo, E. (1929) *La montagna e le leggi per la bonifica integrale*, «L'Alpe», **no.1**, 5-13.

Lazzarini and F. Vendramini, *La montagna veneta in età contemporanea*, Rome, 11-23.

Lunardoni, A. (1904) *Vini, Uve e Legnami nei trattati di commercio*, Rome.

MAIC (1915) *Relazione sull'Azienda del Demanio Forestale di Stato*, Rome.

Maganzini, I. (1911) *Sulla sistemazione dei bacini montani*, «L'Alpe», **no. 5-6**, 252-253.

Manni, D. (1618) *Trattato della direzione dei torrenti*, Pistoia.

Mengotti, C. (1816) *Idraulica fisica e sperimentale*, Venice.

Merendi, A. (1926) *Politica forestale e realtà*, «L'Alpe», **XIII**, no.8.

Miliani, G. B. (1926) *Linee direttrici della politica forestale*, «L'Alpe», **XIII**, 7.

Ministry of National Economy, *Relazione sull'Azienda del Demanio Forestale di Stato*, Rome, 1927.

Morelli, A. (1961) *La tecnica dei rimboschimenti in Sardegna*, in *Atti del congresso nazionale sui rimboschimenti e la ricostituzione dei boschi degradati*, Accademia Italiana di Scienze Forestali, Florence, 217-223.

Muzzi, S. (1955) *Dalla legge forestale del 1877 alle odierne direttive di economia montana*, «L'Italia forestale e montana», **no. 6**, 262-270.

Muzzi, S. (1970) *Vicende storiche della scuola forestale Italiana*, in *L'Italia forestale nel centenario della fondazione della scuola di Vallombrosa*, Accademia di Scienze Forestali, Florence, 350-391.

Nico, P. (1879) *Sulle condizioni forestali della Francia, relazione letta al club scientifico di Vienna il 27 Marzo 1879 dal barone A. Seckendorff*, «Nuova Rivista Forestale», **II**.

Orlando, G. (1969) *Progressi e difficoltà dell'agricoltura* in G.Fuà, *Lo sviluppo economico in Italia. Storia dell'economia Italiana negli ultimi cento anni*, III, Milan.

Osti, G. (1913) *Appunti per uno studio sistematico della legislazione forestale*, «L'Alpe», **3-5**, 83-89.

Pampaloni, T. (1878) *La nuova legge forestale italiana*, «Nuova Rivista Forestale», 97-118.

Panegrossi, T. (1955) *La situazione della popolazione alpina in Italia e la legislazione a favore dell'economia montana*, «L'Italia Forestale e Montana», **X**, 5, 225-239.

Patrone, G. (1952) *Il contributo dello Stato e degli Enti alle sistemazioni montane e al miglioramento e all'ampliamento dei boschi e dei pascoli dal 1867 al 1950*, L'Italia forestale e montana, 321-349.

Patrone, G. (1970a) *Cenni di geografia economica forestale,* Florence.

Patrone, (1970b) *Il contributo tecnico scientifico della scuola forestale italiana dal 1869 al 1924*, in *L'Italia forestale nel centenario della fondazione della scuola di Vallombrosa*, Accademia di Scienze Forestali, Florence, 12-13.

Pavari, A. (1926) *Le sistemazioni montane e i rimboschimenti*, In *L'Italia Forestale*, Florence, 161-191.

Raffaelli, T. (1997) *Dalla repressione del "danno pubblico" alla produzione del "bene pubblico": cultura economica e politiche forestali (1861-1915)*, in *Il Pensiero Economico Italiano*, **5**, no. 2, 41-79.

Romanelli, R. (1990) *L'Italia liberale*, Bologna.

Romano, D. (1986) *I rimboschimenti nella politica forestale italiana*, «Monti e Boschi», **no. 6**, 7-12

Savastano, L. (1893) *Il rimboschimento nell'Appennino meridionale*, Napoli.

Segala, G. (1883) *A proposito del trattato di rimboscamento e di inerbimento delle montagne*, «Nuova Rivista Forestale», **VI**, 159-171.

Segala, G. (1910) *La sistemazione dei bacini montani ed i criteri per compierla*, «L'Alpe», **no. 5**, 129-133.

Serpieri, A. (1926), *L'Ambiente economico e sociale*, L'Italia Forestale, Florence.

Serpieri, A. (1931) *La legge sulla bonifica integrale nel primo anno di applicazione*, M.A.F., Rome.

Surell, A. (1842) *Etudes sur les torrents des Hautes Alpes*, Paris.

Tella, G. Di *Appunti sulle lezioni di Correzione dei Torrenti, tenute dal Prof. G.Di Tella nel R.Istituto Forestale di Valombrosa, anno 1911*, Biblioteca della Sezione di Assestamento del Dipartimento di Scienze e Tecnologie Ambientali Forestali, University of Florence.

Tella, G. Di (1912) *Il bosco contro il torrente*, Italian Touring Club, Commissione di Propaganda per il Bosco e per il Pascolo, Milan.]

Tella, G. Di (1914) *Rimboschimenti ed opere murarie nella restaurazione dei bacini montani*, «L'Alpe», **4**, 97-106.

Tella,G. Di (1931), *Rimboschimenti ed opere murarie nella restaurazione dei bacini montani*, «L'Alpe», **5**, 241-249.

Tella, G. Di (1934) *Per la montagna italiana - Dalla legge forestale del 20 giugno 1877 alla legge sulla bonifica integrale del 13 febbraio 1933* –XI, «L'Alpe», **1**, 1-3.

Thiéry, E. (1891) *Restauration des montagnes*, Paris.

Trifone, R. (1926) *Direttive della legislazione forestale italiana*, in *L'Italia Forestale*, Firenze, 237-259.

Trifone, R. (1953) *Il vincolo forestale prima e dopo la legge del 1877*, Annali dell'Accademia Italiana di Scienze Forestali, **1**, 61-76.

Trifone, R. (1957) *Storia del diritto forestale in Italia,* Accademia Italiana di Scienze Forestali, Florence.

Venditti, N. (1916) *Il problema idraulico e la sistemazione delle acque*, «l'Alpe», **10**, 293-299.

Viviani, V. (1681) *Discorso intorno al difendersi dei riempimenti e dalle erosioni dei fiumi applicate ad Arno in vicinanza della città di Firenze*.

Erosion processes and past climate conditions in the inner lower Alentejo, southern Portugal

Maria José Roxo

e-GEO - Centro de Estudos de Geografia e Planeamento Regional [Research Centre for Geography and Regional Planning], Faculdade de Ciências Sociais e Humanas, Universidade NOVA de Lisboa

Abstract

Research into the extreme climate phenomena of the past, together with analysis of the cartography of soil use and occupation, was a key element to understanding the current state of ecosystem decay in the region of southern Alentejo, Portugal. Information was collected on weather conditions and extreme phenomena (droughts, floods, storms, blizzards) published in regional newspapers (*Bejense*, *Mertolense*), from the mid-nineteenth century up to the first decade of the twentieth century, as well as quantitative data recorded at weather stations from 1883-1884, when these stations were installed in the region (district of Beja, village of Mina de S. Domingos). In terms of cartography, the analysis was based on the agricultural land use map, produced at the end of the nineteenth century for the whole country under the coordination of Gerald-Pery. Our conclusions were reinforced by the results of water-based soil erosion monitoring between 1961 and 1992. Particular attention was paid to the information covering the municipalities of Mértola and Serpa, as they represent vast areas with high degrees of both soil degradation and biodiversity loss (desertification). Climate data associated with the changes in the use of land with different soil-types and of different sizes allowed us to draw conclusions regarding the dynamics of the water-based erosion process and to establish the phases during which the ecosystems suffered greater pressure. This knowledge facilitates the validation of future scenarios around current climate change.

Keywords: extreme weather events, land use, soil degradation, desertification

Introduction

Past soil erosion is one of the main causes of the desertification we see today in the Iberian Peninsula, as well in the Mediterranean region (Brandt and Thornes, 1996; Geeson *et al.*, 2001; Imenson, 2012). One of the most threatened regions in Portugal is Alentejo, in the south, where the land has been degraded by erosion in the past. The threat persists today with the greatest erosion occurrences due to agricultural practices and destruction of scrubland.

According to Imenson and Curfs, "*Natural rates of soil erosion are generally very slow (a few mm or cm per hundred years). Many of the processes that are responsible for erosion are seldom observed because more than 90 percent of the erosion occurs during short and often unpredictable periods of time, when it is not pleasant or even sometimes unsafe to be outdoors*" (2006: 6). Earth scientists are concerned with the consequences of extreme climate events, as it is known that the risk of erosion has been altered by human activities. Changes in land-use and practices may increase or reduce erosion impacts depending on the circumstances.

The purpose of this chapter is to identify extreme climate events that occurred in the southern region of Alentejo, especially in the municipalities of Serpa and Mértola, between the nineteenth century and the first decade of the twentieth century. Using historical descriptive sources, quantitative data from the Mina de S. Domingos weather station and old land use maps (Feio, 1998), we will identify the frequency of events and the impacts produced both in society and in natural ecosystems in terms of land-use and land management systems. In the last part of the chapter, we present the results of the monitoring of water-based soil erosion between 1961 and 1992, which supports the analysis of those impacts.

The above municipalities are located in Lower Alentejo, Southeast Portugal. They are considered marginal rural areas. The particular climate, topographic and edaphic characteristics of the landscapes in these areas makes them of critical to minimal suitability to develop rational and productive agriculture activity. Serpa, Mértola and the inner southern region of Alentejo have a Mediterranean continental climate, with high rainfall and extremes of temperature, an extremely dense dendritic drainage pattern and very poor schist soils that have minimal to non-existent agricultural capacity (Roxo, 1994) (Figure1).

Figure 1. Study area, Serpa and Mértola Hills, *baldio* (common lands), localization

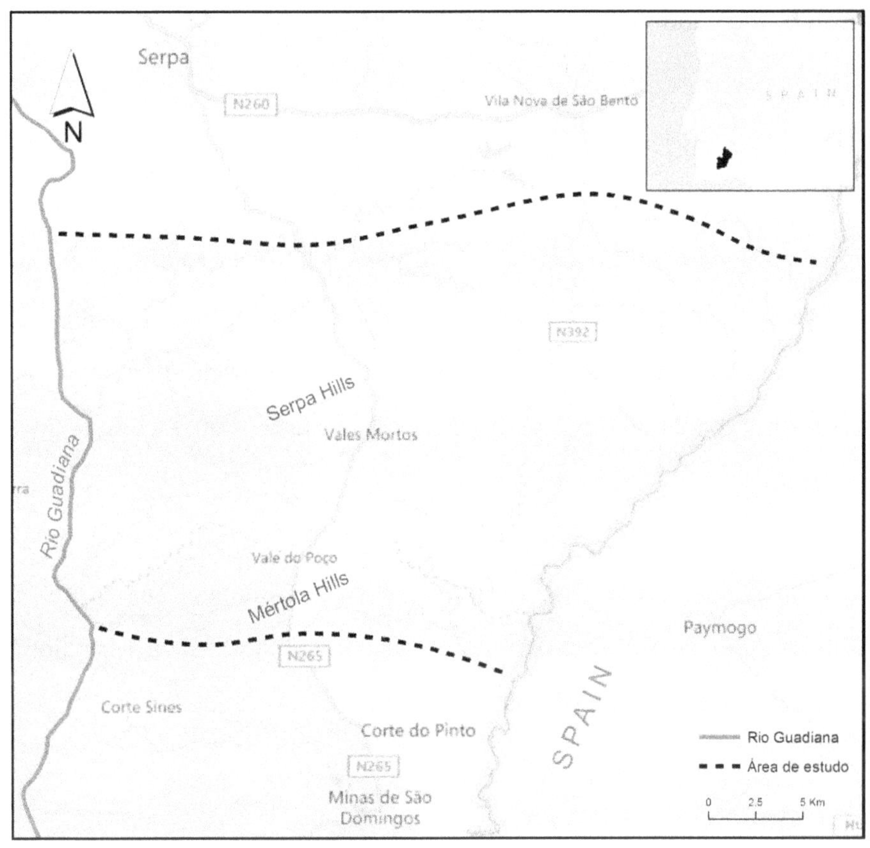

Extreme weather events such as droughts, floods and heavy rains are recurrent phenomena in Alentejo's Mediterranean climate. These extreme phenomena greatly contribute to the soil degradation, loss of productivity and loss of biodiversity.

Most of the research on this kind of phenomena is based on data from scientific measuring instruments. However, in order to understand past climate conditions one also has to use records which are not from instruments (proxy-data) i.e. those supported by descriptive sources.

It is important to note that scientific observations of climate phenomena in Lower Alentejo (municipalities of Serpa and Mértola) only began in the late nineteenth century (1883-1884), at the meteorological station of Mina de S. Domingos, with the recording of rainfall, temperature and wind strength. All the knowledge on the regional climate, which was available up to then, was therefore qualitative, originating from descriptive reports, newspapers, archive documents and chronicles. In terms of availability of sources for research on historically extreme weather events, two periods can be identified: (i) a descriptive period (from 1860), based on qualitative documentary sources, and (ii) a numerical period (1883-1910), based on quantitative, regular and rigorous records from a calibrated weather station.

Results

The analysis of events that occurred in the second half of the nineteenth century and in the twentieth century suggests a regional increase in the frequency and intensity of extreme climate phenomena (droughts and wet periods). There was an increase especially in the severity of the impacts of these phenomena, with direct consequences for soil erosion and land degradation.

Historical analyses reveal that there were major changes in terms of land-use and ownership in these two municipalities during this period. This was due to a government policy that led to the division of common land.

i) Extreme climate events

Comprehensive research was carried out to identify and analyse the contents of the main newspapers published in the second half of the 19th century in Lower Alentejo. The weekly periodical *O Bejense*, first published in April 1860, was analysed from that date up to 1897. Organised in themes and with a network of correspondents spread around other areas in Lower Alentejo, it provided information to the province. This included weather forecasts, reports of extreme weather events and their impact on the land, as well as on the built infrastructure. The consistency of this data was a key-factor towards building a reliable chronology and producing a themed analysis. Other important aspects that strengthened the value of this qualitative information were their regularity and the highly descriptive character of the news.

Over 1,700 copies of the periodical were examined covering a period of thirty-seven years (1860-1897). The gathering all this information, whilst treated with suitable caution, allowed the determination of climatic characteristics of each year. The analysis established the periods of droughts and floods, as well as identifying the good and bad agricultural years. From this analysis, it was possible to detect several wet and dry periods, with drastic social and economic consequences (Table 1). News such as the following provides a good picture of the situation at that time:

"The Guadiana river invaded the village of Mértola. According to the latest news, warehouses on the left bank are covered by the waters. In the village opposite the river, the flood covered the houses of the municipality.

The water rose from the river bed to the square, maybe to twenty-two meters (...). Areas invaded by the water are above the 1822 mark." (O Bejense, December 9, 1876)

In the period under consideration, thirty floods were registered. The heaviest occurred in 1865, 1876 and 1895. Droughts, on the contrary, seem to be less frequent. The worst happened in 1863, 1867-1868 and 1875.

Rainfall data from the meteorological station of Mina de S. Domingos were compared with news from O *Bejense* for the period 1883-1897. The flood that occurred in 1895, for example, was the result of very high rainfall, an annual total of 785mm when the annual average for the period 1883-1910 was 486mm. From 1897 up to 1910, it is possible to identify other wet years, for instance 1902-1903, with an annual total of 684mm and 1907-1908 with 672mm as well as dry years such as 1904-1905 with only 337mm. The excess or deficit of rain had consequences for agricultural production and for the dynamics of the ecosystem.

Table 1. Wet and Dry Periods between 1860-1897

Years	Wet periods	Dry Periods
1860	December	
1861		
1862		
1863		April to May
1864	November	
1865	January	
1866	March and May	
1867 1868		October to December February to May
1869		
1870		September to November
1871		
1872	January and February	
1873		
1874		
1875		January to June
1876	December	
1877	January	
1878		
1879	November	
1880	May	
1881	January and April	
1882		
1883	March and May	
1884		
1885	February and April	
1886	March	
1887		
1888		
1889		
1890		September to December
1891	January and November	May to September
1892	January and May	
1893		September to November
1894	December	
1895	January, February November	May to November
1896	December	
1897	January	

ii) Incentive policies to increase cereal production

The nineteenth century was a decisive period for agricultural development in Alentejo region (Fonseca, 1996). The ideals of economic development and liberalism had political influence over the agricultural production system. Consecutive policies and measures were applied aiming to promote the real growth of agriculture, this crucial economic sector, and some of these policies and measures had a significant (drastic!) impact on the land.

Large areas of land around the main settlements belonging to religious and charitable institutions as well as to municipalities and parishes were purchased by private owners and seen as potential land for agriculture. The abolition of feudal-like rents released a lot of land to agricultural development. However, the most important measures were definitely the ones enforced by central government policies, such as the development and expansion of transport; the rise of markets for agricultural goods from rural areas; and a clear political intention to promote agricultural production and economic development.

In 1882, as clear evidence of the full commitment of the public authorities towards developing agriculture, a national survey was organised to assess the real potential of Portugal's land resources for agriculture. The result was the *Carta Agrícola,* the land registry of agricultural property. High priority was given to the Alentejo region due to its geographical characteristics, and a full description of the different crops and different land-uses was made. This was turned into several 1:50 000 very detailed and valuable maps.

In what became known as Elvino de Brito's law of 1899, legislation was also passed which covered the protectionism of cereal production. This led to huge transformations in the landscape, as farmers responded to the legal stimulus and started to plough thoroughly and clear away natural forest and vegetation (Reis, 1993).

Land left uncultivated was no longer seen as a resource to be kept as it was and rationally managed as before. On the contrary, it was seen as a sign of agricultural backwardness and had to be transformed into productive land through farm implement.

Incentive policies to increase cereal production were followed by political and social pressure to divide the common lands *(baldios*) which still existed. The eastern side of the

Guadiana river still had poor, uncultivated, common land, accounting for approximately 40,000ha in the Serpa municipality and 9,660ha in the Mértola municipality. In 1906, in Serpa, the land was divided into 5,464 small farms (6 hectares each), and in 1926 in Mértola it was divided into 2,610 small farms of different dimensions (Figure 2). Although this land was *baldio*, it had always been important for its resources, such as specific plants, bees' honey and wax, since the Middle Ages (Table 2).

Figure 2. Plots (identified by number and letter) (Roxo, 1994)

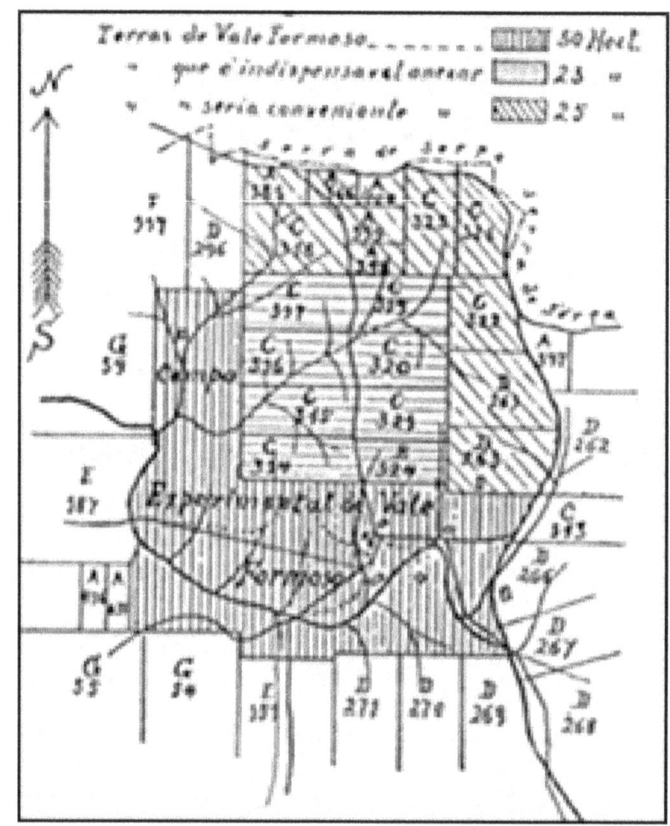

The division of common land into small farms at the beginning of the twentieth century resulted in a widespread increase in land ownership and in the degradation of previously existing natural vegetation (Table 2). It also resulted in the acceleration in the process of soil erosion due to ploughing in shallow soils and on steep slopes.

Table 2. Land Use – *baldio* (commons lands) in the Serpa and Mértola hills
Source: *Carta Agrícola* 1891/1892

Land use	Area (ha)	%
Cereal	2 835	5.3
Natural pastures	935	1.8
Oak woodlands	85	0.2
Shrubs	49 145	92.7
Total	53 000	100.0

This total includes unproductive land (roads, paths, etc.) which represents a residual area of the hills.

The persistence of government policies advocating agricultural growth and technological development, mainly through cereal production and livestock, lead to the first wheat campaign in 1929. This was three years after Salazar took charge of the government and installed a military dictatorship (Rosas, 1994; Lains, 2003).

From the early 1930s to the late 1960s, consecutive campaigns to promote wheat and assist farmers in producing it turned the inner Lower Alentejo into an area of cereal monoculture. According to Roxo *et al.* (1996: 118): "*Intensive agriculture depleted the soils, leading to a massive use of fertilizers; the intensification, later coupled with mechanisation that rapidly became common in the region, contributed to further soil degradation mainly with structural destruction*". The decline in soil productivity was a the result of several factors: (i) soils had no agricultural potential and were not adapted to the kinds of crops used; (ii) the topography of the land (with steep slopes), together with the lithology (metamorphic rocks), promoted intensive overland flow, which quickly eroded the shallow topsoil; and (iii) vast areas of bare soil exposed to local climate conditions contributed to the loss of both volume and fertility.

The consequences in this part of the Alentejo region were a high degree of destruction and degradation of land resources. This turned soil erosion into a serious environmental problem.

iii) Long term monitoring of soil erosion caused by water – Vale Formoso Erosion Experimental Centre (VFEEC), Mértola

The VFEEC was established in a dry cereal-cropped area, with severe soil erosion problems. The soil erosion has arisen from the edaphic and climate characteristics mentioned, as well as from the implementation of the wheat campaigns.

The setup and installation of the VFEEC by Ernesto Batista de Araújo[i] in 1960 was considered a priority by the government authorities due to the condition and degree of soil degradation in the Mértola and Serpa hills. The Centre was seen as fundamental in the implementation and dissemination of soil conservation practices and techniques. Its aim was to carry out intensive and thorough monitoring and gather information: the first data available was from the 1960-1961 agricultural year (September-August).

The VFEEC 18 experimental plots are similar to those used by Wischmeier (1957, 1958) in his experimental studies to obtain the universal soil loss equation. Each plot has a length of 20.0 metres and a width of 8.33 metres, which corresponds to a rectangular surface of 166.6 square metres and is approximately 1/60 of one hectare. Plot 7X is the only one with the same length but half the width (Figure 3).

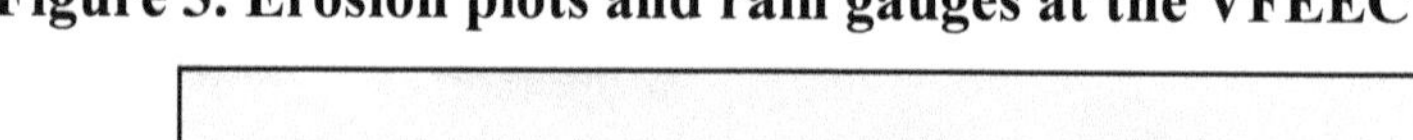
Figure 3. Erosion plots and rain gauges at the VFEEC

[i] Agronomist at the General Directorate for Hydraulics and Agricultural Engineering.

One of the main objectives behind the installation of the VFEEC was to understand the phenomenon of erosion caused by water. Specifically the work set out to analyse the correlation between the *shape*, *intensity* and *duration* of rainfall events and the visible effects of erosion, dependent on a range of crops and soil covers. This would determine and detect periods where there was a greater risk of soil erosion.

The data presented in Table 3 clearly show the impact of agricultural practices on soil degradation and the effect of policies that favoured the production of cereals. These consequences were aggravated by the occurrence of extreme climate phenomena, such as droughts and wet periods. From the research done on the nineteenth century, it appears that there were more references to wet periods than dry ones, which means that there were more conditions where land degradation processes were likely to occur.

Table 3. Maximum values of soil loss – Period 1961/1992

Cover/ Land use	Kg/ha
Natural Vegetation	186
Cereal / Wheat	4 000
Bare soil / plough "up and down"	12 000
Bare Soil / plough in contour lines	5 000

(Roxo, 1994)

The data analyses done by various authors (Rosa, 1982, 1989; Roxo, 1990, 1994; Tomás, 1992) lead to several research conclusions, namely:

i. Wheat production, in the manner it was carried out, clearly and steadily leads to physical soil degradation, and thus to a loss of soil fertility. Mean soil loss per year is 2.5 tonnes per hectare, per year.

ii. The period during which soil loss is more significant is the rainy season (Autumn-Winter), coinciding with, and in some cases dependent on, the farmers' calendar and their cycle of soil movement tasks (burning stubble and ploughing).

iii. Extreme events such as years with droughts and floods cause different types of soil degradation, depending on the physical and chemical proprieties of the soil;

iv. The influence of the slope is not as important as expected. The really important issue is the relationship between the degree of slope and how exposed the slope is, depending on the type of rainfall events.

v. The water erosion process is definitely influenced by the relationship between rainfall intensity, angle of incidence (influenced by wind speed), the direction (weather types) and duration (type of events). Exposure to the air mass is crucial in the process.

vi. The type of arable crops used (dry cereal crops) definitely contributes to the soil degradation process. Land cover and land-use systems affect the soil degradation.

vii. Vegetation (species, cover ratio, etc.) has a fundamental role in protection and for soil preservation. It is a key element in soil erosion caused through the actions of water.

viii. Soil preparation along contour lines (across the slope), as opposed to along the slope, reduces soil loss by less than half.

ix. Pastures based on leguminous species and clovers are more effective in conserving soil.

x. Stubble cover conserves the soil and therefore should not be burnt. This is still a common practice.

xi. Abandonment of agricultural land leads to the clear and steady reduction in soil erosion. This is proportional to natural vegetation recovery, depending on the state of degradation at the time of abandonment.

Final remarks

The present chapter illustrates the potential of descriptive sources, especially when reliable numerical sources are unavailable. It also illustrates the importance of establishing the link between these types of data and cartography and other sources, such as experimental soil erosion yield, to understand the past. Considering the experimental data presented in Table 3, it appears that soil erosion was less in the second half of the nineteenth century than in the 1920s, at the beginning of the Wheat Campaign. In fact, in the 1890s, the soil was still protected by the natural vegetation that covered the common land in the Serpa and Mértola hills (Table 2).

In Alentejo, agriculture was and still is the major factor responsible for environmental degradation and desertification. The consequences can be summarised as follows: (i) massive land-abandonment and emigration; (ii) extensive exposure of rock outcrops due to the total loss of topsoil in vast areas; (iii) decrease in groundwater recharge; and (iv) loss of biomass production and a decrease in biodiversity.

Finally, the current environmental problem in most of the Lower Alentejo region, and especially in the Serpa and Mértola municipalities, is desertification, which is related to land resources (soil, water and vegetation). This phenomenon can be interpreted as a progressive decrease in the self-regeneration capacity of the natural system, where the input-output balance will result in a gradual loss of productive capacity. The problems experienced are the undeniable result of the application of policies that only focused on the economic aspects in the wrong places. Examples of mismanagement of land resources and unintended human impacts resulting in land degradation are numerous. They often reflect the inadequacy of these policies to specific environmental conditions, such as the occurrence of extreme climate events.

References

Brandt, J. and Thornes, J. (1996) *Mediterranean Desertification and Land Use*, Chichester, Wiley.

Feio, M. (1998) *A evolução da Agricultura do Alentejo Meridional: As Cartas Agrícolas de G. Pery: As difíceis perspectivas actuais na Comunidade Europeia*, Lisbon, Colibri.

Fonseca, H.A. (1996) *O Alentejo no Século XIX: Economia e Atitudes Económicas*, Lisbon, Imprensa Nacional.

Geeson, N.A., Brandt, J. and Thornes, J. (2001) *Mediterranean Desertification: A Mosaic of Processes and Responses*, Chichester, Wiley.

Imenso, A. (2012) *Desertification Land Degradation and Sustainability: Paradigms, Processes, Principles and Policies*, Malaysia, Wiley-Blackwell.

Imenso, A. Curfs, M. (2008) "Soil Erosion", LUCINDA Project, http://geografia.fcsh.unl.pt/lucinda/booklets/Booklet%20B1%20EN.pdf

Lains, P. (2003) New Wine in Old Bottles: Output and Productivity Trends in Portuguese Agriculture, 1850-1950, *European Review of Economic History*, **vol.** 7, nº 1, pp. 43-72 .

"O Bejense" – Semanário 1860-1897, Beja.

Reis, J. (1993) *O Atraso Económico Português em Perspectiva Histórica: Estudos sobre a Economia Portuguesa na Segunda Metade do Século XIX, 1850-1930*, Lisbon, Imprensa Nacional.

Rosa, C.A. (1982) Estudo comparativo em talhões experimentais de erosão de cereais, forragens e pastagens - Vale Formoso in *«Pastagens e Forragens»*, **Vol.3**, s.l., pp. 7-20.

Rosa, C.A.. *et al* (1989) O talhão experimental de erosão e sua contribuição para a conservação do solo, Lisbon, MAP, DGHEA, pp. 2-8.

Rosas, F. (1994) *O Estado Novo (1926-1974)*, Lisbon, Estampa.

Roxo, M.J. *et al.* (1990) Autumn rainfall and red schist soil erosion - the 1989 extreme event, presented to the seminar "*Interaction between agricultural systems and soil conservation in the Mediterranean belt*", Lisbon, European Society for Soil Conservation.

Roxo, M. J. (1994) *Acção antrópica e o processo de degradação de solos – Serra de Serpa e Mértola*, Ph. D. dissertation on Environment Natural Resources Management, Lisbon, Faculdade de Ciências Sociais e Humanas, Universidade Nova de Lisboa.

Roxo, M.J, Casimiro, P., Soeiro de Brito, R. (1996) Inner Lower Alentejo Field Site: Cereal Cropping, Soil Degradation and Desertification in Brandt, J. & Thornes, J. *Mediterranean Desertification and Land Use*, Chichester, Wiley, pp.111-133.

Roxo, M.J. and Afonso, O. (2008) Drought Events in Southern Portugal from the 12th to the 19th Centuries: Integrated Research from Descriptive Sources, *Natural Hazards*, Springer, Vol. 47, nº 1, pp. 55-66. (DOI 10.1007/s11069-007-9196-0).

Tomás, P. M. (1992) - *Estudo da Erosão Hídrica em Solos Agrícolas Aplicação à Região Sul de Portugal*, Master dissertation on Hydraulics and Water, Lisbon, Instituto Superior Técnico, Universidade Técnica de Lisboa

Prehistoric and medieval mobile pastoral strategies in the Mediterranean: an archaeo-zoological perspective

Marta Moreno-García [1] and Carlos M. Pimenta[2]

[1]Instituto de Historia, Centro de Ciencias Humanas y Sociales, CSIC - Consejo Superior de Investigaciones Científicas [Spanish National Research Council], Spain

[2] Direcção-Geral do Património Cultural [Directorate-General for Cultural Heritage], Portugal.

Abstract

Traditionally, seasonal pastoral systems as transhumance have been interpreted as the 'natural' husbandry strategy to be followed in the Mediterranean world. Underlying this situation was the assumption that topographical relief and season were, if not totally determinant, primary factors in the emergence and development of mobile pastoral strategies. The general idea is that environmental conditions rule the economy and society of the human communities in this geographical region. However, with the increase in palaeo-environmental studies, particularly pollen and charcoal analyses, this statement has become questionable. Since mountains in the Mediterranean are too low to grow alpine meadows, open summer grazing areas would not be a 'natural' feature of this landscape. Upland pastures can be considered mainly the product of human interference, either by fire and axe or through grazing (Mellars, 1976; Forbes & Koster, 1976). Before extensive clearance took place, accessibility to and herding in woodland pastures during the summers may be assumed to have been difficult. Furthermore, because wooded zones existed in the lowlands this may have been unnecessary. Thus, it appears that the role played by environmental conditions in the emergence of seasonal mobile pastoral systems in this geographical area could have been less than initially thought.

Keywords: archaeo-zoology, environmental change, transhumance

Introduction

Studies among traditional Mediterranean pastoral communities (Lewthwaite, 1983; Barker & Grant, 1991) have shown that periodical movements of livestock offer the possibility of maintaining larger populations during those seasons when local grazing resources are scarce. Consequently, physical conditions of a geographical area regarding grazing availability must be considered together with the scale at which livestock might have been kept. Both variables are linked. Equally valuable and closely related to them is the question of the extension of the territory exploited. Intra- or extra-regional movements could distinguish transhumance from other mobile pastoral systems. Finally, it cannot be forgotten that all these issues are associated with the level of productivity pursued by those pastoral human groups.

From prehistoric times up until nowadays there have been multiple pastoral strategies in the Mediterranean, some of which are possible to trace in the archaeological record. The aim of this paper is to discuss the possibilities offered by the study of archaeo-zoological remains to explore some of the issues mentioned. The absence or presence of particular age groups and the recognition of lambing and killing seasons were examined from data analysis which may help to recognise the pastoral systems followed.

Regarding husbandry practices in the past

In communities of hunter-gatherers, animals are valued for the resources their dead carcasses provide. These are known as the primary products: meat, fat, skin, feathers. Even their bones and teeth were used as raw material to manufacture implements or adornments. With domestication, a big change took place. Animals could be exploited for the resources they provided while alive, the so called 'secondary products' (Sherratt, 1981; 1983): their power to push a plough, a means for transportation, their dung to fertilize agricultural fields or to be used as fuel. In the case of the caprines, their wool was used for textiles plus their milk, and in the case of domestic birds, the eggs were a product.

It is important to note that primary products and most secondary products can be stored, moved and exchanged so production seems to be an essential variable to take into account when analysing husbandry practices. Diversification or optimization of production are equally key issues (Halstead, 1996; 1990). Within a subsistence economy, as the one that would have existed in prehistoric times, animals would tend to be kept for a variety of purposes. Diversification is one of the devices employed by self-sufficient societies to cope with unforeseen circumstances. For the small-scale farmer specialisation on a single resource would have been a risky strategy.

The availability of grazing areas must have been one of the major concerns for herders at all times. Exploitation of local pastures resulted in two patterns of husbandry practices. One was sedentary in which animals were kept in the same grazing area the year around, with provision of leaf or grass fodder for the winter months; and another one, in which grazing areas located in the plains were best exploited during warm, wet winters, and mountain pastures offered livestock an escape from hot dry summers. The altitudinal variations between lowlands and uplands and the differing temperatures and rainfall caused a displacement of annual productivity peaks within both ecosystems.

French human geographers at the beginning of the twentieth-century, distinguished between three mobile systems of livestock exploitation: *i*) nomadism, *ii*) transhumance and *iii*) pastoral life of the mountain (Fribourg, 1910; Arbos, 1923; Vidal de la Blache, 1926). In nomadism, the entire human group accompanies the flocks and herds all year around within a system of free-range pastures. There are neither fixed settlements nor permanent agriculture. In transhumant systems, it is only part of the community, the shepherds, who are engaged in pastoral activities. The rest of the group is sedentary and agriculture is predominant in these communities. The shepherds move away from their permanent base, only for part of the year, to make use of seasonally complementary ecological zones when they are most productive. The last system refers to those seasonal movements of livestock, which simply involve short-distance journeys between the lower and higher parts of the same mountain slopes. Animal feeding resources are found at two different ecological levels but within the same territory.

Transhumance and pastoral mountain life, identified as mobile pastoral systems in the Mediterranean, diverged from nomadism in the fact that they were closely associated to agriculture. It should not be forgotten that in rural economies animal husbandry and agriculture are two elements that go together. In short, different mobile pastoral strategies have been followed over time depending on the availability of grazing areas, the scale of herding and the diversification or optimization of production.

Two archaeo-zoological case studies

Cova de Els Trocs (Huesca, Spain)

The cave is located in the central Pyrenees at 1564 m a.s.l. The interior is cold with an average temperature ranging from 6° to 8° C. Relative humidity is around 98%. Excavations have been conducted since 2009 by a team of archaeologists from the University of Valladolid (Rojo Guerra *et al.*, 2011). Three occupation surfaces dated to the Early Neolithic were identified.

The composition of the large and medium-sized mammal remains recovered is dominated by ovicaprines, particularly sheep. Their contribution ranges from 80% to 91% in each of the three levels. Hunted species, represented by red deer, roe deer, wild boar or hare and wild animals such as the bear that could have lived in the surroundings are very scarce.

Such faunal composition demonstrates that the human community inhabiting the cave was highly engaged in pastoral activities and that most faunal remains derived from human consumption. The ovicaprine kill-off pattern shows that 78% of the remains belong to animals of less than 1½ years of age. Among these many are from foetal and neonate individuals. Few adult animals are present. Such profile indicates that animals were breeding on site, an event that most likely occurred during the spring or early in summer. This result is corroborated by the presence of spring-summer migratory birds (*i.e.*, the Great Spotted Cuckoo or the Barn Swallow) and of birds that can be found at this altitude, like the Quail and the Crag Martin, only during this season. From a palaeo-ecological point of view, the charcoal evidence and the occurrence of the Red Squirrel and the Fat Dormouse together with birds closely associated with woodland indicate a landscape rich in forests with some open grazing areas. All-in-all, the pastoral strategy followed by this group may be identified with an altitudinal seasonal movement which aimed to explore the most productive ecosystems during the year. Meat and probably milk were the products exploited.

The archaeological site of Castillo de Albarracín (Teruel, Spain)

The castle is located within the walls of the town of Albarracín in Teruel. It stands at 1195m a.s.l. in the Sierra de Albarracín. The site was excavated by a team of archaeologists from Teruel in the 1990s. Our study focuses on material collected from two large well stratified dumps dated from the eleventh- to the fourteenth-century AD (Moreno-García, 1999). The first three chronological periods correspond to the Islamic occupation whereas the last two are Christian. The material may be identified with table refuse.

The largest number of remains was recovered from periods one and three. Ovicaprines constitute the dominant species (over 70% of the mammals). Their relative abundance decreases from period three onwards, reflecting a change in the consumption of lamb meat over time. During the last Islamic period, such decrease was complemented by the meat of rabbits, whereas during Christian times (four and five) contributions from cattle, swine and red deer increase. This means beef meat, pork and venison were then preferably consumed. In short, this pattern reflects the cultural change that happened within this medieval urban space. Nevertheless, a change in production interests appears to have occurred already within the Islamic community. The ovicaprine kill-off pattern in period one shows two peaks of mortality of young individuals and animals in their prime while that from period three is dominated by mature animals of five to six years of age and even animals older than eight years. If flocks were kept to provide meat and milk in period one, in period three the priority was to keep mature animals for their wool. Such husbandry strategy is only possible if grazing areas are available. Given the fact that spring and summer pastures are the best in Sierra de Albarracín, it may be argued that keeping flocks that specialised in wool production was only possible if they were taken away during the winter months. Such a strategy is closer to the practice of transhumance in the sense previously defined.

Conclusion

Human communities within the same physical environment transform the landscape as a response to cultural, social, political and economic circumstances. From the Neolithic onwards, agriculture and animal husbandry have been two activities that changed natural environments. Archaeology provides us with different temporal windows to understand how, when and why these changes took place. In particular, faunal remains are an important body of data to identify the role that pastoral strategies might have had in environmental change through time.

References

Arbos, P. (1923) The geography of pastoral life. *The Geographical Review*, **13**, 559-575.

Barker, G. & Grant, A. (1991) Ancient and modern pastoralism in Central Italy: an interdisciplinary study in the Cicolano Mountains. *Papers of the British School at Rome*, **59**, 15-88.

Forbes, H.A. & Koster, H.A. (1976) *Fire, axe, and plow: human influence on local plant communities in the southern Argolid*. In: Dimen, M. & Friedl, E. (eds.) Regional variation in modern Greece and Cyprus: toward a perspective on the ethnography of Greece, *Annals of the New York Academy of Sciences*, **268**, 109-126.

Fribourg, A. (1910) La transhumance en Espagne. *Annales de Géographie*, **19**, 231-244.

Halstead, P. (1990) Present to past in the Pindhos: diversification and specialization in mountain economies. Archeologia della pastorizia nell' Europa Meridionale, *Rivista di Studi Liguri*, **56**, 61-80.

Halstead, P. (1996) Pastoralism or household herding? Problems of scale and specialization in early Greek animal husbandry. *World Archaeology* **28** (1), 20-42.

Lewthwaite, J. (1983) The art of coarse herding: archaeological insights from recent pastoral practices on west Mediterranean islands. In: Clutton-Brock, J. & Grigson, C. (eds.) *Animals and Archaeology 3. Early herders and their flocks*, Oxford: BAR International Series **202**, 25-37.

Mellars, P. (1976) Fire ecology, animal populations and man: a study of some ecological relationships in prehistory. *Proceedings of the Prehistoric Society*, **42,** 15-45.

Moreno-García, M. (1999) The archaeo-zoology of transhumance in medieval Spain. Unpublished PhD thesis, Department of Archaeology, University of Cambridge, Cambridge.

Rojo Guerra, M., Royo Guillén, J.I., Garrido Pena, R., García Martínez de Lagrán, I., Tejedor Rodríguez, C., Arcusa Magallón, H., Peña Chocarro, L. & Moreno, M. (in press 2011) La Cueva de Els Trocs: un asentamiento del Neolítico Antiguo junto al Pirineo Axial. *Actas do 5º Congresso do Neolitico Peninsular*, Lisbon.

Sherratt, A. (1981) Plough and pastoralism: aspects of the secondary productos revolution. In: Hodder, I.; Isaac, G. & Hammond, N. (eds.) *Pattern of the past: Studies in honour of David Clarke*, Cambridge: Cambridge University Press, 261-305.

Sherratt, A. (1983) The secondary exploitation of animals in the Old World. *World Archaeology*, **15** (1), 90-104.

Vidal de la Blache, P. (1926) *Principles of human geography*. French edition 1921 ed. London: Constable.

Climate Change and Responses of Biological Diversity

D. James Harris

CIBIO - Centro de Investigação em Biodiversidade e Recursos Genéticos [Research Center in Biodiversity and Genetic Resources], Universidade do Porto.

Abstract

Climate is known to be a key determinant of species distribution. Climate, however, is in no way static. In particular, during the Quaternary (2.6 million years ago to the present) climate has fluctuated periodically, with periods of global cooling resulting in the "Ice Ages". At the peak of the last glacial period, around 20,000 years ago, ice sheets would have covered much of North America, Northern Europe and Asia. Clearly very little of the current fauna and flora of the region could have survived there during this period. At the same time, these ice sheets caused other profound effects on other parts of the world, not least dramatic drops in sea levels that allowed terrestrial species to move between previously isolated landmasses. It has therefore been accepted for a long time that biological diversity has been greatly impacted by past climatic changes (e.g. Woodward, 1987). However, recent advances in modelling techniques and the widespread availability of population genetic data have allowed for more accurate scenarios to be drawn, and to make precise predictions regarding future responses.

Keywords: biogeography, genetics, biodiversity, climate change

Introduction

Traditionally palaeo-environmental proxies, such as pollen samples or fossil records, were used to assess historical distribution areas and combined with biogeographical data suggested that many species survived through glacial maxima in lower latitude "refugia" (Huntley and Birks, 1983). However, it was the combination of this evidence, with a phylogeographic approach that revolutionized our understanding of the size, location and effect on the inhabitants of these refugia. Phylogeographic studies use genetic data from various molecular markers - now typically DNA sequences, often of cellular organelles such as chloroplast or mitochondria - to infer relationships between individuals, and then set these relationships within a geographic context. This allows the population history to be traced and interpreted in the light of palaeo-environmental conditions. The two sources of evidence are highly complementary, with fossils for example being used as calibration points for determining rates of evolution of molecular markers, while molecular data can be collected for many organisms that have limited or no fossil records.

Figure 1. The "classic" view of expansion of species from Southern refugia (adapted from Hewitt 1996). Hatched areas show extent of ice sheets and the dotted line maximum extent of permafrost at the last glacial maxima. Arrows indicate typical dispersal routes after climate ameliorations. Often species from the Italian Peninsula were blocked from expansion by the Alps. Biological and genetic diversity hotspots occur in the Southern regions, since only some of the individuals and species from these regions recolonised the North.

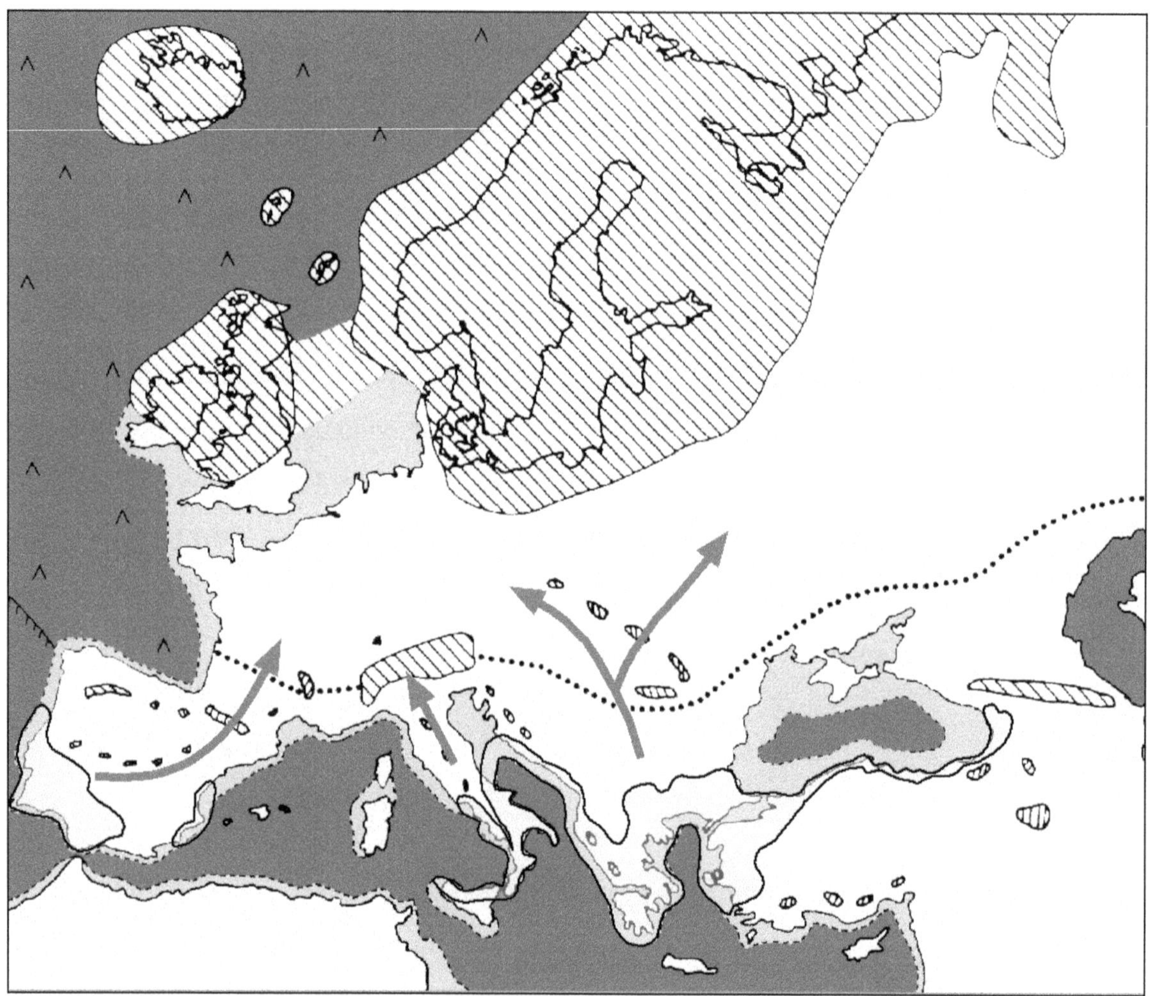

Initially phylogeographic studies often supported the hypotheses of "southern refugia" in Europe, corresponding to the Iberian and Italian Peninsulas and the Balkans, where considerable genetic diversity remained (e.g. Hewitt, 1999). Survivors of glacial periods from one or more of these refugia then re-colonised Northern Europe when conditions improved. One interesting finding was that hybrid zones were often created where colonisers from different refugia met in Central and Northern Europe. Thus while the first assessments identified "Southern richness, Northern Purity", with the Southern refugia hotspots for biological diversity, it became clear that some northern regions could be considered "melting pots" - highly diverse mixtures of lineages from different southern regions (Petit *et al.*, 2003).

As phylogeographic studies became more common, they also increased in sampling density as the costs of sequencing hundreds of individuals became practical for many different organisms, and this led to further refinements to the refugial models. One was the finding of a limited number of "Northern refugia", where isolated populations had survived in presumably very small patches of suitable habitat outside of the southern refugia (e.g. Provan *et al.*, 2005). Another key finding was that diversity was often heavily structured within the Southern Peninsulas. This led to the idea of "refugia within refugia" (Gomez and Lunt, 2007). Many species show this pattern, so that the Europe wide pattern of southern richness and various melting pots of admixture are mirrored within the southern refugia (Figure 2). However, this occurs across an older time frame, since the occupants of these refugia met, mixed and became isolated again in cycles with climatic changes, while current residents of Northern Europe reflect only the last expansion and contact events.

Figure 2. An example of the same process mirrored within a southern refugia. The outline shows the current distribution of the salamander *Chioglossa lusitanica*. Dark patches indicate refugial areas. Individuals from only one refugium expanded to colonize the majority of the current range, and the two forms meet at a melting spot around the Mondego River valley. 95% of all genetic diversity occurs only in the Southern half of the range (adapted from Sequeira *et al.*, 2008).

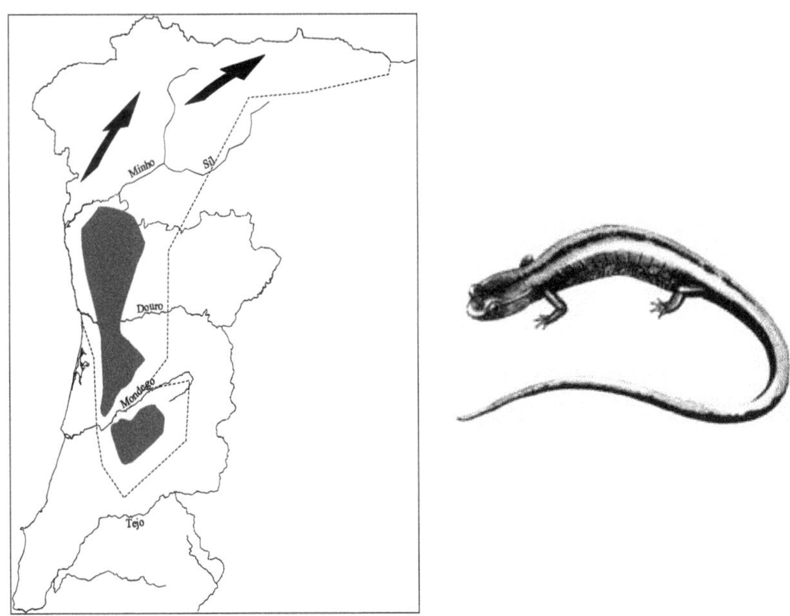

Marine Barrier: The Straits of Gibraltar

As well as expanding sampling within southern refugia, sampling outside of them also led to new understanding of the way terrestrial species could cross what had been deemed insurmountable marine barriers. The Strait of Gibraltar is very deep, and so had been considered a continuous divide between Southern Iberia and North Africa since the Miocene (from about 23 to 5.3 million years ago) (e.g. Hewitt, 1999). It was even used as a calibration point in early phylogeographic studies, a known division around 5.3 million years old separating terrestrial taxonomic groups found on both sides. Finding limited genetic (mitochondrial DNA) diversity between various species in the Iberian Peninsula and North Africa, such as chameleons and tortoises, was considered as evidence of their recent, human-aided, introduction to the former (e.g. Harris *et al.*, 2003). However, genetic assessments of various taxonomic groups across the Strait indicated that a simple vicariance pattern, that is the splitting of a group of organisms by a physical barrier to dispersal, did not fit the data in most cases. In particular, the unexpected finding of relatively recent colonisations of two snake species from North Africa to Iberia led to a reconsideration of the Strait as a permanent barrier (Carranza *et al.*, 2006). Lower sea levels would have narrowed the Strait during the last glacial maxima (between 26,500 and 19,000–20,000 years ago), leading to several small islands emerging that could have acted as stepping-stones between the continents, leading to a noticeable North African flavour to the fauna and flora of the Iberian Peninsula. It also highlighted the advantages of comparing fossils with phylogeographic data, as fossils of one of these snakes, *Malpolon monspesullanus*, were known from the Iberian Peninsula from much earlier. Presumably, snakes have colonized Iberia, gone extinct in an earlier glacial period, and then recolonized in the last glacial maxima, thus demonstrating the fluid movement of species, even in the presence of a considerable geographic barrier, to respond to climate changes. It also showed that it is often hard to determine whether or not species are anthropogenically introduced. The Egyptian mongoose and the common genet were both traditionally considered as introduced to the Iberian Peninsula (Gaubert *et al.*, 2011). Genetic data did support the hypothesis of human introductions for some species, including Barbary Apes and the common genet. However, some such as the snakes and the Egyptian Mongoose appeared to all have actually crossed naturally. The native status of others, such as the tortoise, remains unresolved; they may have been introduced by very early human activity but probably crossed naturally around 30,000 years ago based on recent assessments of faster-evolving microsatellite markers (Gracia *et al.*, 2013). What is clear is that not all species show the same pattern of colonization, and that stochastic effects are extremely important.

Genetic Markers

The fact that some early phylogeographic assessments were misinterpreted, or at least were very imprecise, is related to the numbers of markers used in early studies, almost all of which relied on mitochondrial DNA in studies of animals. For relatively recent events, such as the case of the tortoises in Iberia, this single marker is not variable enough to give precise dates of colonisations to separate anthropogenic from natural colonisations. In other cases, it can be completely misleading, since it is maternally inherited. For example, in hares the mitochondria from the Mountain Hare is found in many other hare species in the Iberian Peninsula (Alves *et al.*, 2003). Although the closest extant mountain hares are in the Alps, during the last glacial maxima they occurred much closer in the Pyrenees. Some interbreeding took place, and mitochondrial DNA of Mountain Hares became common in many populations of other hares, particularly in the Northern part of Iberia, either due to random effects of genetic drift or through selection. Sampling only mitochondrial DNA would give a completely misleading picture of species distribution patterns in this case. As more markers are applied in phylogeographic studies similar findings of "mitochondrial introgression", that is of mitochondrial DNA from one species in individuals of another, are becoming common, and highlight how no single method is infallible when trying to reconstruct complex historical movement patterns.

Species Distribution or Niche Modelling

Just as the introduction of phylogeographic analyses radically altered our understanding of species responses to past climate change, so is the new tool of species distribution modelling. Also called niche modelling, the methodology infers the geographical areas suitable for a species to occur under varying environmental conditions (Guisan and Zimmermann, 2000). Such models are often used to investigate the impact of climate change on species distributions. Essentially the range of climatic conditions under which a species can exist are modelled, and compared with climatic scenarios to estimate the range of the species as the climate changed. Models of past distributions can be compared to phylogeographic or palaeo-environmental data to validate results. Pollen cores or palaeo-botanical data are particularly valuable for this, as fairly precise historical distributions for various plant species are known across multiple time frames. Prediction of unknown distributions of species can also be tested through fieldwork. For example, models predicted isolated populations of Wall Lizards in North Africa from where there were no records of this species. These were then confirmed through targeted surveys (Kaliontzopoulou *et al.*, 2008). Thus these models, despite many assumptions and limitations, can certainly be useful in some circumstances. Not only this, but unlike the other methods, forecasts can be made for how species will respond to future climate changes. These are, of course, much more difficult to validate.

Conclusion

Various different methods can be used to assess how biological diversity responds to climate change. Each has different strengths, and integrative approaches are clearly the most powerful. Climatic fluctuations have been continuous during the Quaternary, and species have shown remarkably fluid responses in their distributions in response to this. However, these cycles have been much slower than some predicted scenarios for future climate changes. Furthermore, different species behaved very differently to past changes, making it very difficult to determine how future distribution patterns will be for individual species. On the other hand, each methodology is continuously being improved upon, so that more and more accurate predictions of past, current and future distribution patterns can be made.

References

Alves, P.C., Ferrand, N., Suchentrunk, F. & Harris, D.J. (2003) Ancient introgression of *Lepus timidus* mtDNA into *L. granatensis* and *L. europaeus* in the Iberian Peninsula. *Molecular Phylogenetics and Evolution*, **27**, 70-80.

Carranza, S., Arnold, E.N. & Pleguezuelos, J.M. (2006) Phylogeny, biogeography and evolution of two Mediterranean snakes, *Malpolon monspessulanus* and *Hemorrhois hippocrepis* (Squamata, Colubridae), using mtDNA sequences. *Molecular Phylogenetics and Evolution*, **40**, 532-546.

Gaubert, P., Machordom, A., Morales, A., Lopez-Bao, J.V., Veron, G., Amin, M., Barros, T., Basuony, M., Djagoun, C.A.M.S., San, E.D., Fonseca, C., Geffen, E., Ozkurt, S.O., Cruaud, C., Couloux, A. & Palomares, F. (2011) Comparative phylogeography of two African carnivorans presumably introduced into Europe: disentangling natural versus human-mediated dispersal across the Strait of Gibraltar. *Journal of Biogeography*, **38**, 341-358.

Gomez, A. & Lunt, D.H. (2007) *Refugia within refugia: patterns of phylogeographic concordance in the Iberian Peninsula*. In: Weiss, S. and Ferrand, N. (eds) *Phylogeography of Southern European Refugia*. Springer, Dordrecht, NL.

Gracia, E., Gimenez, A., Anadon, J.D., Harris, D.J., Fritz, U. & Botella, F. (2013) The uncertainty of late Pleistocene range expansions in the western Mediterranean: a case study of the colonization of south-eastern Spain by the spur-thighed tortoise, *Testudo graeca. Journal of Biogeography*, **40**, 323-334.

Guisan, A. & Zimmermann, N.E. (2000) Predictive habitat distribution models in ecology. *Ecological Modelling*, **135**, 147-186.

Harris, D.J., Znari, M., Mace, J.C. & Carretero, M.A. (2003) Genetic variation in *Testudo graeca* from Morocco estimated using 12S rRNA sequencing. *Revista Espanola Herpetologia*, **17**, 5-9.

Hewitt, G.M. (1996) Some genetic consequences of ice ages, and their role in divergence and speciation. *Biological Journal of the Linnean Society*, **58**, 247-276.

Hewitt, G.M. (1999) Post-glacial re-colonization of European biota. *Biological Journal of the Linnean Society*, **68**, 87-112.

Huntley, B. & Birks, H.J.B. (1983) *An atlas of past and present pollen maps for Europe 0-13,000 years ago*. Cambridge University Press, Cambridge, UK.

Kaliontzopoulou, A., Brito, J.C., Carretero, M.A., Larbes, S. & Harris, D.J. (2008) Modelling the partially unknown distribution of wall lizards (*Podarcis*) in North Africa: ecological affinities, potential areas of occurrence, and methodological constraints. *Canadian Journal of Zoology*, **86**, 992-1001.

Petit, R.J., Aguinagalde, I., de Beaulieu, J.L., Bittkau, C., Brewer, S., Cheddadi, R., Ennos, R., Fineschi, S., Grivet, D., Lascoux, M., Mohanty, A., Muller-Starck, G.M., Demesure-Musch, B., Palme, A., Martin, J.P., Rendell, S. & Vendramin, G.G. (2003) Glacial refugia: hotspots but not melting pots of genetic diversity. *Science*, **300**, 1563-1565.

Provan, J., Wattier, R.A. & Maggs, C.A. (2005) Phylogeographic analysis of the red seaweed *Palmaria palmata* reveals a Pleistocene marine glacial refugium in the English Channel. *Molecular Ecology*, **14**, 793-803.

Sequeira, F., Alexandrino, J., Weiss, S. & Ferrand, N. (2008) Documenting the advantages and limitations of different classes of molecular markers in a well-established phylogeographic context: lessons from the Iberian endemic Golden-striped salamander, *Chioglossa lusitanica* (Caudata: Salamandridae). *Biological Journal of the Linnean Society*, **95**, 371-387.

Woodward, F.I. (1987) *Climate and plant distribution*. Cambridge University Press, Cambridge UK.

Walling and barriers: protection from the weather in nineteenth-century Portugal

Cristina Joanaz de Melo

Instituto de História Contemporânea [Contemporary History Institute], Faculdade de Ciências Sociais e Humanas, Universidade NOVA de Lisboa

Abstract

This chapter considers reactions to unexpected, extreme, weather conditions in the Portuguese territory throughout the nineteenth century. It analyses legislative and governmental as well as local responses to natural hazards caused by unpredictable excessive rainfall as much as by drought. These opposing conditions produced devastating impacts for people, cattle, agricultural land, and infrastructure. Water-management systems had to be developed. However, in the context of the Liberal Regime, state action was strictly tied by private property rights.

It is argued that, under a political ideological liberal framework, common property rights blocked Public action towards the implementation of preventive policies against flooding across all the country. The difficulty in finding political solutions to justify the building of water-management systems on private land forced local action to be taken. The rural communities, the highlanders and the fishermen were pushed to develop their own strategies for sheltering from and protecting against natural hazards. However, the constructions erected because of local pressures, were seen by the political elites as being harmful to the natural watercourses. Therefore, the "ignorant" were to be blamed and were responsible for the rivers flooding.

Nevertheless, ultimately, both local and traditional strategies were revealed to be more efficient under emergency pressures than public/ educated solutions that only started to arrive by the mid-1880s. These protective works proved to be vital for local communities, both wealthy and modest landowners, who faced a particularly harsh century regarding rainfall, the extent of torrential floods and destruction of food supplies.

Keywords: drought, barriers, floods, insulation, protecting, rainfall, walling, weather, water-management systems.

Under debate: historiography following historical traps?

Until very recently, in the 1990s and 2010s, most historians were driven by their interests in looking at the management of countries through the most significant economic trends and mainstream economic activities of the nineteenth century: the industrial revolution, developments in agriculture, creation of new transports networks or science and technology. For many decades, historians considered the huge palette of other resources, landscapes and economic systems, beyond the ones that characterized the enclosure movement or mining activities and the iron-steel industry, as marginal objects of research.

However, these other topics such as, commons and heaths, became the target for historical evaluation mainly after the publication in 1990 of the seminal book *Governing the Commons* by Elinor Ostrom. This took place in parallel with studies on climate and policies on territorial management.

From the point of view of environmental approaches, there has been a greater interest in analysing the uses and importance of *other resources* of the commons taking into account the perspective of tensions between private and common property. As well as this development, from 1990 onwards, the analysis of natural resources outside the legislative legal framework for property has consistently become the target of environmental research among many historians (Zagli, 1996; Warde, 1998; Bevilacqua & Corona 2000; Agnoletti 2002, Smout, 2000, Rotherham & Agnoletti, 2010). These interdisciplinary studies about landscapes examine how materials and resources of low economic value, in the Modern era up to the late nineteenth century, became valuable and object of profits and dispute. The natural resources that were not covered in the "industrial revolution" have begun to be integrated in studies on policy and territorial management alongside the other resources.

Following this framework of analysis one can observe that issues like climate change, weather impacts, natural disasters, recovering and restoring landscapes and their influence in political decision making for managing territories, have already been scrutinized in a significant amount of manuscripts. Some of the examples from studies in the period 1990 to date, which look at nineteenth-century Europe are listed here: Zagli, 1996; Agnoletti, 1999, 2005; Hall, 2005; Warde, 2002, Vivier, 2002; Coronna, 2008; Rotherham, &, Agnoletti, 2010; Agnoletti & and Hall, 2011; Barca, 2010; Corona, 2011.

This chapter uses the cross-thematic approach and interdisciplinary analysis and methodology found in the studies mentioned above. From the thematic as well as the methodological point of view, this chapter aims to contribute to the historiography debate with a cross-thematic approach on the impacts of extreme weather events to trigger economic activities that can be identified in a specific geographical context, place, and in a given chronology. Although the hypothesis raised in this chapter could be extended using a comparative perspective with other constitutional regimes in Europe, this study considers a single geographical case study, Portugal. However, it will occasionally pinpoint a few comparative aspects with other European cases just to emphasize the relevance of some crucial ideas.

A range of sources are used to study the problem of how weather impacts of extreme violence are relevant to both natural resources of low economic value as well as to forgotten landscapes with their lack of economic value for farming and mining. These sources include parliamentary debates, legislation, and technical and scientific reports from the1800s. The secondary bibliography was chosen to include environmental, economic, and medicinal history as well as studies in ethnography and anthropology.

Public action: encompassing needs and the possibilities of intervention

Developing the general theory of climate change, issues like global warming, mini ice ages, melting of the polar ice-caps, similar rainfall in the mountains and in the lowlands, torrential floods, or extreme droughts, became objects of historical analyses, both in the USA and in Europe. Seminal works such as those of Lambert (1982), or Grove and Rackham (1988/2001), cover periods from the medieval times to the present. Following on from these, in the 1990s and 2000s, environmental historians, using climate data, have stressed weather and climate tendencies as crucial factors in understanding the causes of natural hazards that occurred in Europe throughout the nineteenth century.

Under this perspective, authors like Christian Pfister analysed climate series from 1500 to 2000, inspiring historical analyses of environmental policy-making for the circum-alpine region. Based on climate data, the author, and a few other historians, has proposed that the effects of flooding (between the 1830s and the 1870s), due to an increase in rainfall, triggered the momentum for rulers deciding to take action.

However, throughout the 1800s, the political rulers in almost all of the European nation-states invoked mostly economic, social and also political factors to postpone environmental policies to protect against natural hazards. The delays in the necessary, political decision-making in these sectors resulted mainly from four obstacles. These were firstly, rulers had focussed their priorities on the building of the transport networks (waterways, railways, and roads in the era of the boom in the iron-steel and textile industries, Hobsbawn (1975). Secondly, there was the resistance of the highlanders to the privatisation of the commons, which were coveted for pasturage by private landowners, provoking conflicts and social instability in the same mountainous regions where afforestation was being advocated (Whithed, 2000; Melo, 2011). Thirdly, and maybe the worst reason of all, was the ignorance of politicians compared to the knowledge of engineering bodies, which created a deep gap in understanding over the real possibility of controlling water hazards (Branco, 2005; Melo, 2010). Fourthly, there were external factors such as the instability of the frontiers in the mountains during the period of nation-state building in Europe.

The changes in the political process were happening at the same time as the majority of most episodes of severe rainfall, hailstorms and flash floods / landslides across the European territories (Whithed, 2000). Adding to the geopolitical reorganisation of Europe (Miquel 1998; Montanelli 2004), epidemics spread across all Europe from Russia to Portugal, from the 1830s to the 1870s (Baldwin, 1999; Saavedra, 2010; Brantz, 2011, Almeida, 2012, 2013). There were also internal blocking vectors for planning water and civil protection policies. In France, the Italian States, Portugal and Spain, conflicts between the state authorities and the highlanders emerged due to the central public attempt for afforestation of the slopes.

At the beginning of the nineteenth century in Portugal, neither the local populations nor its rulers were capable of interpreting the unexpected amount of precipitation as becoming the new pattern of rainfall for many years to come. This was similar to what was happening in the rest of the European regions suffering from an increase in rainfall throughout the 1800s (Pfister, 1984, 2002). The records of the changes were the personal memories of parents and grandparents, rather than statistical data. Consequently in 1823, from 1835 to 1837, and in 1843, the large-scale flooding of the rivers Mondego and Tagus [figure 1 refering to the map of the Inberian Peninsula] were considered exceptional, both in extent and frequency (Pfister, 2000). The same applied in the case of tributaries of the Tagus such as the River Dgebe, which served the city and fields of Évora and flooded from 1852 to 1858.

However, through the second half of 1800s, these kinds of events developed from occasional to quite regular, and became increasingly devastating. Extremely violent sea inundations occurred in the western continental Portuguese coast from 1848 to 1852, as frequently as the rivers burst their banks between 1852 and1857, and 1859 to 1861 and later on, in the period 1874 to 1877. Heavy hailstorms occurred throughout the 1860s but also caused significant damages to the crops. In the Portuguese territory, from the 1850s onwards, particularly in the most acute periods of extreme rainfall from 1855 to 1857, and again in 1859 and 1861, the population of the low-lying plains was perishing in an Armageddon-like scenario. The increasing torrential devastation, led to the spread of epidemics, lack of food and starvation.

If excess of water was a very difficult issue to deal with, severe droughts were an additional problem. Such extreme events occurred in Portugal in the 1860s, early 1870s and more frequently throughout the decade of the 1880s (Melo, 2010). In the 1850s and early 1860s the Portuguese newspapers on rural topics, widely debated the problem of a surplus of water in agricultural areas. However, in 1865, a wealthy landowner in the Province of Alentejo, D. Miguel de Alarcão, triggered the discussion about the opposing problem: how to overcome the unusual problem of extremely scarce water supply throughout the year. Such a situation took place, for example, in 1863. In order to prevent similar events like those of the previous year, D. Miguel built ditches, tanks and irrigation channels on his properties at his own expense. Even then, that strategy was not sufficiently efficient to provide the necessary water supply for agriculture, people and cattle.

Figure 1: Relief Map of the Iberian Peninsula

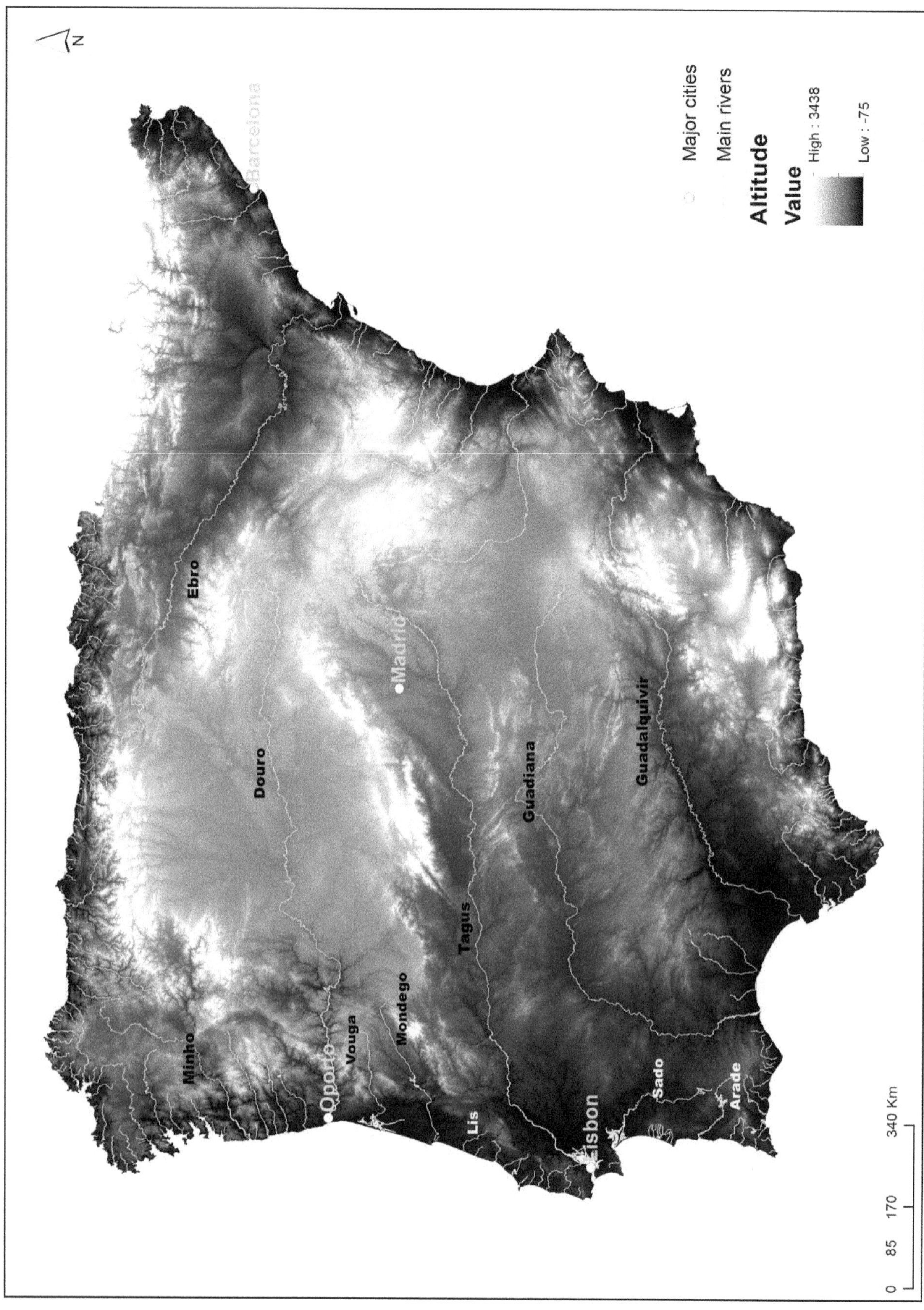

[Authorised by Daniel Alves; source: SIGMA Sistema de informação geográfica e modelação de dados aplicada à História de Portugal e Atlas - Cartografia Histórica http://atlas.fcsh.unl.pt]

Furthermore, unlike the rest of Europe, the Portuguese kingdom did not face any threat in internal-national political implosions. Still in the 1860s, and despite the climatic pressure of the previous decade and the availability of scientific and technical know-how on watershed restoration and water-management engineering (Magalhães, 1861, 1864; Valladas, 1865; Eça, 1872, 1877), decision making for environmental policies was put aside by the executive and legislative powers. Territorial management was still driven by other sectors, which were considered more important than afforestation and water policies, particularly the transport network[i].

One might easily understand that politicians would hardly consider spending huge sums of public or private money on land of no economic value, such as mountain summits, slopes, terraces or heaths. This was especially so when there were more attractive investment opportunities in transport or the textile industry and when productive land was being affected by both devastation and disease. Understandably, the view was that public works should be focused there.

Even though weather impacts had resulted in public disasters, which meant that local populations had to be rescued from life threatening situations until the mid-1850s, the aforementioned phenomena continued to be considered as occasional by the Portuguese political elite. Consequently, the policy followed on catastrophic weather hazards was to treat those, which by default would be rare, acute public crises, with no further thinking about planning preventive actions to avoid a repetition of the effects of future crises. Therefore, populations with their lives, cattle and belongings in danger, would require nothing more than circumstantial and localized help from the government. This help would be provided in very few areas of the country specifically to cover their major or minor needs (Melo, 2010).

For the two decades of the 1850s and 1860s, even though powerful landlords were represented in the legislative forum (some as members of Parliament), they continued to witness the loss of their sources of wealth due to the abnormal intensity of hailstorms, torrential rainfall, floods, high sea-tides and hurricanes around the coast, and were powerless to intervene. They were even unable to convince the other parliamentarians

---

[i]Almeida, J. V. De (1899) *"A Febre dos caminhos e ferro tem-nos distrahido a atenção d'outras obras importantes"*[The trains fever has been distracting us from other important works] in *Chronica agrícola*, in *Agricultura Contemporânea. Revista Agricola e Agronomica*, **37,** 37-40.

about the level of destruction in agriculture and communications due to floods, in the surrounding countryside of Lisbon served by the river Tagus. Actually, during the period from January to March 1855, the Baron of Almeirim[ii] described the flooding of the farmed fields in the lowlands of the Tagus River as the living 'Apocalypse'. According to him, water-management systems were crucial for the survival of the population, to avoid cattle drowning, and, even more importantly, to create the conditions where the crops of that and the following years could thrive. This was occurring in the farms of the regions of Santarém and Golegã distant from the capital fairly from 50km to 80 km, following up by the river.

Yet, it was only by the end of the spring of 1855, that the parliamentarians became fully convinced of the extent of the crises in agriculture and food shortages due to the rainfall and flooding. Some of them tried to speed up the legal process for beginning water-management systems in the Mondego watershed. The first piece of legislation had been presented for approval in the Chamber of the Deputies in 1853. Despite the moves to approve such legislation, the government and legislators saw their intentions blocked, once again, by the dogma of inalienable private property rights.This attitude started to change slightly in favour of some environmental programmes from 1855 onwards, due to repeated apocalyptical scenarios of public disaster. These were repeated and aggravated, year after year, over the period from 1855 to 1857 in agriculture and health, and again, between 1859 and 1861[iii].

However, the approval of large-scale public water-management systems kept being delayed. This was largely due to the fact that liberal politicians, who had implemented the premise of inalienability of private property rights in the 1830s, were not mentally prepared for voting laws which could hinder those prerogatives. Accepting a general law that would allow the State to manage watersheds across the country, equally over private, common and State properties, would in their view amount to treason.

Therefore, in the mid-1850s, when the political elites were confronted with the need to go from circumstantial help to preventive actions, other obstacles emerged. Political decisions

---

[ii] Barão de Almeirim [Baron of Almeirim], 03; 05; 07 .02.1855 e 03.05. 1855, 1855 in *Diário da Câmara dos Deputados*, Fevereiro 1855.

[iii] (1877) *Annaes do Observatório do Infante D. Luís. Resumo das Principais Observações Meteorológicas Executadas Durante o Período de 20 Annos Decorridos Desde 1856-1875*, Lisboa Imprensa Nacional.

towards constructing a network of water-management infrastructures were blocked by the uncertainty of the legislative and territorial scope of state intervention over private and common properties (Melo, 2010).

The conquest of general property rights by the liberal regime in Portugal, in the 1830s, tied up public policies towards territorial management, even in the contexts of public disasters. Not surprisingly, the difficulties listed previously were being felt in other similar constitutional liberal regimes, such as France, Italy and Spain. They had equivalent laws concerning property rights, and were dealing with similar restraining factors, to approve national water-management policies (Agnoletti, 1999; Calvo, 2001; Derex, 2004; Melo, 2010).

In fact, the required water-management networks were put on hold until 1884 and 1886, when the parliamentarians and the Government, finally approved national regulations for water flows - watersheds, streams, rivers and lakes (Pato, 2008; Amorim, 2008; Melo, 2010). These regulations were applied equally across private, common and public property, for the first time since 1832. Ancient rights regarding water management had been abolished and no liberal laws replaced them.

Thus, within the periods of severe water hazards, from 1852 to 1861 and also from 1875 to1877, while politicians were discussing legislative affairs about the limits of State intervention on private properties, local populations were confronted with particularly harsh conditions regarding torrential rainfall and floods. In order to minimize the negative impacts of extreme weather occurrences, the inhabitants of the regions at risk built the structures needed to protect themselves and their lands from flooding (as shown later) even where those solutions would alter the river's natural course.

Indeed, in 1860, in the Tagus, the protection of the river margins was being developed by private endeavour. Landowners had kept on strengthening banks and river margins by constructing stone walls or fencing them with trees[iv]. Meanwhile, in the 1850s, and again in the 1860s, populations were suffering from devastating torrential downpours. These occurred in the lowlands near to the coast which was also subjected to the sea's high tides

---

[iv] Money compensation given to the landowners that had built the protections in the river margins of the Tagus river. Order from the Minister of Public Works, 22th of February of 1860 to the Civil Governor of the District of Santarém 1860, *Diário de Lisboa* de 24 de Fevreiro, nº44, 1860.

and unexpectedly inland in the highlands, around the area of the Tagus. Near the border with Spain, people, dragged down by the currents, were drowned in the floods. In Parliament even the Minister of Public Works, Tiago Ponte e Horta reported such horrendous episodes to justify his extreme concerns about the lack of proper policies towards the torrential downpours and flooding[v]. His view was that different solutions from those already being pursued ought to be developed by the central authority.

In the course of this decade, scientific opinion makers would support their arguments through using the rural press. According to João de Andrade Corvo, future Minister of Public works these kind of occurrences kept on being aggravated because the weather was behaving differently from former seasonally *normal*/ known manifestations of rain and temperature[vi]. If weather conditions that favoured all those hideous circumstances could not be controlled, their effects could nonetheless, be technically minimised. At the very least, health and agriculture demanded immediate attention. Water-management systems should be constructed. However, when legislative and political obstacles seemed to have stopped, other obstacles had to be overcome.

In the period 1855 to1857, the country was facing a crisis with food shortages, an inefficient supply of imported goods, health problems and increased mortality. Politicians had to turn their attention to the horrendous panorama of general famine (with crops devastated by torrential floods), malnutrition, and disease spreading in wet environments, favoured by non-existent sewage systems.

As a vast amount of literature on economic, political and health history has already demonstrated (Branz, 2011), policies facing public disasters in the nineteenth century were not topics voluntarily included in any political programme. Neither were they a chosen priority for any government in Europe, ranging from the Austrian Empire to the British Isles or to the Iberian Peninsula. Thus, it was within a very harsh context of the developments of pandemics in Europe (Baldwin, 1999) which had parallels in Portugal between 1856 and1858 (Cascão, 1999; Saavedra, 2010; Almeida, 2013), that finally, the

---

[v] Tiago da Ponte e Horta, 01.02.1861, Summary of the Session of the Chamber of the Deputies, in *Diário de Lisboa*, 1 de Fevereiro de 1861, **280**.

[vi]Soares, R. de M. (1865-66) *Chrónica* Agrícola, in *Archivo Rural*, vol. VIII, **359**; Idem (1865) *Um velho proprietário e pequeno Lavrador, Comunicado* in *Archivo Rural*, vol. VII, **637,** 636-638; Idem, (1867) *Chronica Agrícola*, in *Archivo Rural*, vol. IX, **135**.

Portuguese politicians were confronted with the need to think about water as a priority in the country's management.

In order to plan, the country's complex geography had to be mapped, but first it had to be discovered. Rainfall data had been consistently recorded only since 1854 and the first map of the Portuguese watersheds would not be completed until the following decade. Misunderstanding of geography had already jeopardised, the building of the Este railways lines on the Lisbon – Évora route near to the border with Spain[vii].

Managing unknown territory: lack of geographical data

Portugal features a wide diversity of contrasting climates distributed through a myriad of landscapes. This territory is a mixture of Mediterranean, Atlantic and continental climates, concentrated in a small area of around 840,000 km^2, distributed across a very heterogeneous topography, from highlands to valleys and floodplains, together with continental, coastal, wet and dry landscapes and a large density of river systems in the mountainous areas.

The country is divided evenly into two major climatic and geomorphological areas by the River Tagus. The northern region is characterised by a very sharp topography of Atlantic climatic influence. The southern region is sub-divided with the part ranging from the Tagus River to the mountains in the inland of the Algarve Province, having a very high Mediterranean climatic influence and the southern region of the Algarve, being a hybrid zone of transition towards the Mediterranean. This sub-region has an Atlantic climatic influence, as seen in its vegetation[viii].

The country also becomes more complex for areas that may be considered "Atlantic Mediterranean" since they combine characteristics of both typologies. The best example is the enclave of "Terra Quente" (Hot land) in the valley of the Douro River (where Oporto wine is produced) in the northern part of the country, in the provinces of Beira Alta and Trás-os-Montes. This region could or should have Euro-continental and Atlantic influences, but Nature has decided otherwise. Another enclave of Mediterranean influence

---

[vii] Tiago da Ponte e Horta, 01.02.1861, DCD, *DL*, Fevereiro, 1861, 280.
[viii] Ficalho, C. de, "*Conferência feita pelo Exmo sr. Conde de Ficalho, director do Instituto Geral de Agricultura e professor da Escola Politécnica de Lisbo*" in *Revista Agrícola,* Tomo V, 3ªa série,5-8.

is located south of Lisbon, along the coast in the "Serra da Arrábida", an upland promontory over the sea, where the Mediterranean vegetation lies literally over the Atlantic. The land receives salty and cold-water high tides along the shore or in the dunes. Sometimes, the rain regime that in Mediterranean mountains would be torrential heavy downpours concentrated in short periods, here tends to be more prolonged (Ribeiro & Daveau 1987).

If excessive rainfall can be problematic along the coast and to the north of the Tagus River, the southern region between this river and the Algarve, and the mountains of the "Serra da Estrela" range (north of the right bank of the Tagus River), can suffer from extreme droughts more frequently than the other areas (Ferreira, 2006). Being far from the sea, lack of water or combined hot temperatures and humidity potentially lead to the degradation of potable waters and the spread of mosquitoes and diseases (Saavedra, 2010).

Thus, when torrential rainfall increases and water floods over the riverbed margins, the fields are trapped between two masses of water: the swirling currents from the mountains and the maritime waters, meeting in *the middle* of the floodplain areas (Ferreira, 2006). However, in the 1850s and 1860s this knowledge was not available for the decision makers to plan their policies towards water management. In some areas of the country, floods and droughts were expected annual phenomena. That is why the significant hazards posed by the water were so difficult for parliamentarians to grasp. Not only were they extreme but also they occurred much more frequently. According to the memories of the elderly, the rainfall season was lasting a lot longer *than before*.

Between 1854 and 1858, when Governments realised the need to plan sanitary policies and civil protection, the tools available were either imperfect or non-existent (Melo, 2010). The full reconnaissance of the country was performed by public cabinets of the Ministry of Public Works Commerce and Industry between 1852 and 1882[ix]. Production of the overall

---

[ix] Branco, R. M. C. (2005) *The Cornerstones of Modern Government: Maps, Weights and Measures and Census in Liberal Portugal (19th century)*, Thesis Submitted assessment with a view obtaining the degree of Doctor in History and Civilization from the European University Institute, Florence, August; (1868) *Relatório da Arborização Geral do País*, Lisboa, Imprensa Nacional; (1865) *Relatório da Direcção Geral dos Trabalhos Geodésicos, Chorográficos, Hydrográficos e Geológicos do Reino no Anno de 1863-1864* in *Boletim do Ministério das Obras Públicas Commércio e Indústria*, 8, Agosto, Lisboa, Imprensa Nacional, 166-175; (1871) *Trabalhos Geodésicos, Topográphicos, Hydrográphicos, e Geológicos do Reino, Executados Desde 1 de Julho de 1868 a Dezembro de 1869* in *Revista das Obras Públicas e Minas,* Tomo II; 23, Novembro, 385-411.

geographic map of Portugal at the scale of 1/ 500 000 was started in 1861 and published in 1865. The map of the distribution of woodlands and trees was designed as an overlay over that map, in 1867. The agricultural layer was initiated in 1882, but it was never finished. Moreover, it was only in 1871, that the Geographical chart, the unfinished constituent parts of the Choreographic Chart, and the map of the distribution of trees were generally distributed to the different ministries and their respective executive Directors of the government departments. So at least until 1871, even the technical offices of the government had no tools for planning and for carrying out work over the country[x]. Thus, the local populations were basically on their own, trying to protect their property and farmed land from flooding or drought.

Considering the response of the public bodies to the population suffering under the impacts of flooding was too slow or inadequate in coping with the unpredictable nature of the severe weather, local populations suffering from this instability had to develop their own strategies to ameliorate the effects. Local sources of materials were necessary for the purpose. The land of wastes (heath and mountain pasture) and of commons, were able to furnish materials adequate to build walls or small dams to sustain river margins, shrubs to make shelters, and stone to build rubble walls or wood to make tools or personal equipment to shelter people, cattle and machinery from the unexpected extreme conditions of the weather.

Local, but effective: craftsmanship, plantations and small water-management systems

In a seminal work with an ethnographic and anthropological focus, Ernesto Veiga de Oliveira, and Fernando Galhano Benjamim Pereira identified several typologies for both housing and shelter all over the country, including the Archipelagos of Madeira and Azores. Huts and sheds built to protect people and cattle from extreme weather conditions would be made from low-value materials, with little isothermal insulation and very plain architecture (Oliveira & Galhano, 1994). Although the authors claim that those structures were quite uncomfortable, they had a crucial role in several economic and human activities. Historical data is available to confirm the ethnological and ethnographic data for building protection systems against heavy rain, floods, cold, and extreme heat throughout

[x] Folque, F. (1872) *Trabalhos Geodésicos, Topográphicos e Geológicos do Reino*, in *Revista de Obras Públicas e Minas,* Tomo II, 23, Lisboa, Imprensa Nacional, **407**, 386- 411, p.407.

nineteenth century Portugal. Some of them concerning storage structures, river margins fencing and logistics for fishing in the rivers, can be even traced back from the twelve to the sixteen centuries in almost all Portuguese watersheds [xi].

Leite (1999) found that in the regions of the Minho and Douro watersheds, stonework, walls, channels and fish-breeding tanks were quite abundant through the nineteenth century. These protective works were repeating ancient strategies in overcoming extreme weather events with the intensity and frequency of phenomena such as hurricanes, hailstorms, torrential flooding and high tides recorded in the nineteenth century, which increased the local demand for building materials. This new and increasing need for fencing, and the parallel growth in demand for natural building resources with low economic value (such as sand, stone, and shrubs or reeds), were apparently becoming more frequent.

Throughout the decade of the 1850s (Leite 1999), structures looking like igloos[xii], walls built along the margins of streams constructed using rubble stonework or in some cases brick, are well documented for the Minho, Douro and Mondego watersheds. This evidence shows that the local populations had to respond to the effects of extremely violent weather on their own much quicker than the bureaucratic and educated elite (Valladas, 1862, 1867; Eça, 1866) understood that natural hazards were cyclical and preventive policies for water management were needed with the utmost urgency. This would happen across all kinds of landscapes: in fertile meadows, farmed areas, windy highlands, wet or sandy areas.

However, the political and scientific elites did not generally accept the locally built structures as refined architecture or effective for managing river-water regimes. These protection systems were considered by the technicians of the ministry of Public Works as well as by their hierarchical superiors, to be the major reason for watercourses changing directions because these solid constructions such as fishing ponds and mills were forcing water to run outside the natural riverbed[xiii]. Barriers (bunds) made of trees or stonework

---

[xi] Coelho, M. H. Da C. (1992), "A pesca fluvial na economia e sociedade medieval Portuguesa" in *Actas do Seminário Pescas e Navegações na História de Portugal (séculos XII a XVIII)*, Lagos, Comissão Nacional para as Comemorações dos Descobrimentos Portugueses, **83, 86,92, footnote 46,91 footnote39, 94,** 81-102.

[xii] Capello. H. and Torres, L.(1883) *Viagem à Serra do Gerez e suas Caldas em Setembro de 1882* in *Boletim da Sociedade de Geografia de Lisboa*, 4ª série, 6, Lisboa, imprensa Nacional, **533,541**, 526-542 ; Sarmento, F. M. (1883) *Expedição Científica á Serra da Estrela 1881*, Lisboa, Imprensa Nacional.

[xiii] Portaria de 24 de Julho de 1854 do Ministerio das Obras Públicas — Diário do Governo n.° 176) mandando destruir algum arvoredo plantado por particulares nas margens do rio Douro, e prejudicial á sua

were erected too deeply into the riverbed in the dry season, and did not take into account the extent of winter floods. Therefore, it was only under the surveillance and technical support of trained officers from the Ministry of Public Works, that these same walls and fences could be installed[xiv].

From the official point of view, the stonework and tree plantations done by the landowners in the riverbeds or along their margins were considered to be outrageous behaviour. The landowners were just trying to appropriate more land for agriculture, breeding fish or enlarge their estates by underhand means so carelessly putting everyone else in danger. Therefore, private landowners should be prosecuted for the consequences of flooding to fertilise the land that resulted in public disasters, and should be heavily fined[xv].

The judicial process moved against the Baroness of Alvaiazere in 1837. The case, which came to an end in 1844, against the aristocrat, is an example of the on-going tension between municipal officers following the Public Works Ministry's orders and private landowners. Public and private entities had very different understandings of river margins and riverbed management. The local authorities of Torres Novas under the order of the Civil Governor of Santarém destroyed the fences erected on the properties of the Baroness, which bordered the Almonda River (a tributary from the Tagus). The public authorities claimed that the barriers made from the trees were affecting the natural river flow and they won the case[xvi].

---

navegação [Ordinance, July 24th of 1854 from the Ministry of Public Works – Order to destroy some trees planted by private landowners on the banks of the River Douro, which are harmful to its navigation].

[xiv] Circular do Ministério do Reino de 21 de Agosto de 1850 aos Governadores Civis, proibindo às câmaras e administradores dos concelhos conceder licenças para construções nas margens dos rios [Ordinance of the Ministry of the Kingdom of August 21, 1850 to the Civil Governors, prohibiting the counties and administrators of the municipalities from issue permits for construction on the banks of rivers].

[xv] "Devem ser mandadas demolir as azenhas, e todas quaesquer outras obras, construidas nos rios e ribeiras, que arruinarem pontes, obstarem à livre navegação e trânsito, ou derem causa à estagnação de águas" [Must be demolished The mills, and all the other works built in rivers and streams, which ruin the bridges and imped the free navigation as well as the traffic, or that have caused the stagnation of water] in Ribeiro, J. S. (1854) *Resolução XII. Obras nos rios e junto a pontes* in *Resoluções do Conselho de Estado* , Tomo I na secção do contencioso Administrativo Coligidas e explicadas por José Silvestre Ribeioro, Lisboa, Imprensa Nacional, **61**, 60-194.

[xvi] Requerimento da baroneza de Alvaiázere contra o procedimento do administrador do concelho de Santarém por ter demolido as árvores que protegiam as suas propriedades nos mouxões do Tejo [Petition from the Baroness of Alvaiázere against the procedure of the county administrator of Santarém for having demolished the trees that protected her properties in the sandislands of the river Tagus], in Diario Government, May 20, No. 118, 1844, Lisbon, 1844, in *Diario do Governo*, 20 de Maio 1884, Lisboa.

This tension among private landowners, municipal authorities and the Ministry of Public Works carried on being a fruitful field of judicial contests, throughout the century. Landowners living by the rivers persisted with the practice of constructing buildings on an *ad hoc* basis. A similar situation that, in turn, was also frequently reported in official records mostly regarding the northern and central regions of Portugal, as in the rivers Cávado, Corgo (Douro watershed), Sore (Tagus watershed), Tagus, Dão (Mondego watershed)[xvii]. Moreover, through the decade of the 1850s and the 1860s, the able Ministers of this sector reinforced and shortened the intervals between direct orders to Civil Governors and from them to the municipal Mayors, to carry out any necessary demolition of the structures and to make sure that the offenders were fined[xviii].

Until the end of the 1860s, this tension between protection of marginal landscapes and obstructing riverbeds due to the construction of several systems for water control would be severely criticised by respectable engineers and MPs. The educated elite and engineers had determined that building structures along riverbanks and in riverbeds by private landowners, who were by default ignorant, was damaging the rivers (Valladas, 1875). The structures were the main cause for the division of flows and silting up of riverbeds[xix].

However, in the middle of this last decade (1860s), the opinions of the ministers of Public Works started to change favourably towards traditional strategies of protection against severe floods. These were the same kind of structures that the public authorities had previously been ordered to destroy and were now to be improved. Protective walls in the riverbed and tree barriers or rubble walls along the banks were encouraged, but to a plan

---

[xvii] Circular do Ministério do Reino de 21 de Agosto de 1850 aos Governadores Civis, proibindo às câmaras e administradores dos concelhos conceder licenças para construções nas margens dos rios [Circular of the Ministry of the Kingdom, August 21, 1850, to the the Civil Governors, prohibiting the counties and the administrators of the municipalities from issuing permits for construction on the banks of rivers]; Portaria do MOPCI de 17 de Janeiro de 1854, expedida ao Governador Civil de Coimbra, para que este averiguasse acerca da regularidade das represas construídas por particulares nos leitos de rios e ribeiros, destinadas a irrigações de campos privados e agisse em conformidade, com a situação. [Circular of the Ministry of Public Works Commerce and Industry, January 17, 1854, to the Civil Governor of Coimbra, in charging him personally to find out about the regularity of permits of the dams constructed by private landowners in the beds of rivers and streams, designed to irrigate private fields and to act in accordance with the situation].

[xviii] Circular do MOPCI de 30 de Setembro de 1864 aos Directores de Obras Públicas para que fizessem publicar as disposições da portaria de 21 de Agosto de 1850, relativas às restrições de construção nas margens dos rios por particulares e respectiva aplicação de coimas [Circular of the Ministry of Public Works Commerce and Industry, September 30, 1864 to the Directors of Public Works ordering them to publish the provisions of the ordinance of August 21, 1850, related to building restrictions on river banks by individuals and fines].

[xix] Ribeiro, J. S. (1854) *Resolução XII. Obras nos Rios e Junto a Pontes* in *Resoluções do Conselho de Estado* , Tomo I na secção do contencioso Administrativo Coligidas e explicadas por José Silvestre Ribeioro, Lisboa, Imprensa Nacional, 60- 194.

that would benefit both the farmed land, and the natural flow of the currents. This type of scheme for protecting the river banks was then to be followed, this was proposed by competent engineering, generally into the 1880s (Loureiro, 1880).

In 1856, the Minister of Public Works instructed the municipal authorities to erect barriers along the banks of the Tagus[xx]. The technical and scientific differences between scientific and local knowledge around building defensive protection systems centred on the distance away from the banks where the structures and barriers needed to be placed (Loureiro, 1875). The materials for the building processes for walling appear to have been quite similar.

In the hills and even mountains, small springs and streams running gently through narrow riverbeds, could easily be tamed and diverted with small water-management systems (Sarmento, 1875). These required manual labour and craftsmanship for the stonework. Redirecting a stream bed would not be difficult in areas where water would gently flow through the natural drainage channel to the end of a valley[xxi]. Yet, unlike in the lowlands where the major problem was a surplus of water, in the uplands, the problem was how to retain water for the summer to compensate for the lack of rainfall. For that reason, building water cisterns and distributing it according to the needs of farming and humans became a skilful, methodical and accurate technology (Valladas, 1862).

These structures were classed as primitive by contemporary actors of the educated elite, as well as within the primary phase of anthropological literature of the nineteenth and twentieth centuries, for their appearance looked irregular and untidy. Those systems were probably extremely efficient for there was little news in the rural press about the highlanders having trouble with water supply, in the District of Viseu, and Guarda, for instance[xxii]. On the contrary, they complained about the lack of woods in the mountains and hills, referring them to the Royal Central Association for Agriculture Affairs who were

---

[xx] Circular do Ministério das Obras Públicas de 3 de Setembro de 1856 ao Governador Civil de Santarém para que se procedesse à construção de sebes e plantações na margem direita do tejo para defesa dos campos nda Golegã, Diário do Governo, de 5 de Setembro, nº10, 1856.
[xxi] Idem, Ibidem; Francisco martins SARMENTO, *Expedição Científica á Serra da Estrela 1881*, Lisboa, Imprensa Nacional, 1883.
[xxii] D. José de Alarcão, *Revista Agronómica*, Terceira série, Tomo III, 1865, 224.

better positioned to access central power, and present their requests[xxiii]. Landscapes and materials could differ across the country, but the concept was the same, using natural materials to maintain a water supply and avoid devastation through rain and flooding.

The inhabitants of inhospitable environments in mountainous or coastal areas achieved positive results in preventing the serious impacts of floods as well as retaining water in the presence of drought (Valladas, 1875). This was done by developing an articulated system for preventing the devastating impacts of inland floods as much as for providing a water supply for human and farming consumption. Thick but permeable barriers were created by raising banks with earth along the margins of streams and planting these margins with bamboos, or placing netted reeds and local shrubs on the margin of the floodplain where the plants would grow up and spread quite rapidly (Valladas, 1875). Therefore, the impact of devastating floods would be reduced while the farmable lands would receive the benefits of irrigation.

In the hilly areas of the Portuguese provinces of Beira Baixa, Ribatejo, Beira Litoral, or Beira Alta, artificial water reservoirs built for a family or a small community would be located on the edge of a cliff, on a very steep area of a slope, as described by Lourenço Costa in his excursion to the Serra da Estrela (Costa, 1875). They were built and placed in these specific areas to resist damage by other water-flows. These cisterns or dams for irrigation or for water storage were strategically placed, next to crags, in steep-sided valleys, or inside riverbeds below waterfalls. Being part of the slope or the cascade systems themselves, they did not constitute an obstacle to the river flow, unlike the water mills or the convent's fish-breeding dams, which were placed in the main river-course where flows were already very large (in the primary water basins, mainly in the lowlands).

Comparing this description with similar structures that are still functioning and used for the same purpose today, for instance in Moimenta do Cabril (Figures 2-3), when artificial small lakes, ponds or dams overflowed, the surplus water would naturally drain out in the valleys through the secondary and tertiary watersheds. There would also be a natural flow through the streams where these constructions were built, in the cliffs and scarps where

[xxiii] *Archivo Rural, Jornal de Agricultura, Artes e Sciências Correlativas,* Lisboa, 1854-1876; *Gazeta dos Lavrdores,* 1880; *Revista Agrícola,* 1866-1876, Lisboa; *Revista Agronómica,* 1858-1864, Lisboa

they were dug or set into the slopes and valleys, and positioned within the inner natural drainage system of the mountains, adjusted to the inclination of the draining slope.

Small cisterns and ditches to both drain water away from farmed areas as well as to irrigate them were also built in hills with little forest which were full of rocky deposits on the slopes and terraces (Figures 2-3). Building these structures was efficient, quick, and did not require huge investment either in materials and labour or in sophisticated technology.

Figure 2. Source:Moimenta do Cabril. photograph Elizabete Rodrigues.

Figure 3. Source:Moimenta do Cabril. photograph Elizabete Rodrigues.

The populations living in the mountainous and hilly ranges would have absorbed the knowledge of how to master water under extreme weather conditions much better than the inhabitants of the lowlands. Living in hostile environments, their default approach to the management of the areas, where they lived and farmed, was well attuned to the conditions. Having few visits from the local authorities, and even less from central authorities, they were compelled to survive on their own. They had to adapt to the environment in which they lived.

For the construction of the water infrastructure as noted, the materials were available locally. Since floods and droughts occurred over a wide variety of terrains, the protection systems would require building materials, which were readily available and existed within easy transport distance. For instance, the resources needed for the building of shelters in the mountains, of huts on sandbanks by the seashore (Brito, 1960) or for walls and fences erected to sustain riverbanks, would differ greatly. Thus, materials were used according to their availability in each area (as discussed later).

With the need for building defences in the majority of the watersheds, it can be supposed that the emphasis on the use of natural resources meant they were becoming products of regular extraction, rather than as in former times just used for small tasks. This can be verified for materials such as stone or sand. This reality was noted in official reports in the Districts of Aveiro in the delta of the river Vouga (Oliveira 1867), a topic which was disregarded by central public authorities. Thus, historical data suggests that from the 1860s onwards, quarried resources and raw materials such as sand, also employed to fuel the pottery industry, were in much wider use than the central administration had expected (Ferreira, 2010).

Later, in 1875, the statistician Gerardo Pery raised this same issue, emphasizing that the quarry industry (limestone, granite, marble and others) was known to be profitable, not only in the previously mentioned regions of Leiria and Aveiro but even more so in the District of Évora, in Alentejo. Yet, there were no official data on the quarry industry (Pery, 1875). However, rocks and stones were used in construction both on the slopes and on the summits of the hills. The shepherds' shelters were mostly made of stone, sometimes covered with hay and reeds, which were impermeable to rainfall. These can be found in the Douro Valley, in the Region of Miranda, on the left bank of the Douro Valley[xxiv] as well as in Serra da Estrela[xxv]. Stonework to build shelters which could hold fires inside for warmth in winter could protect from heat in summer providing shade and cool; some would be covered with special *juncae* (reed). These kinds of plants as well as flax were used for roofs or fences. Since they grew in water, when dry they no longer retain or absorb water, they become impermeable and water runs off them (Morais 1988). These coverings were made to protect against rain, wind or even excessive heat, to produce shade or for keeping cool.

Huts and shelters in the highlands in areas used for pasturing and with a sparse population would be made of materials close at hand: stones, wood, sand and dry mud mixed with stones[xxvi]. In the lowlands, especially in Alentejo, fern (bracken) would probably be

---

[xxiv] Nobre, José António, *Património Rural na Terra de Miranda e Artes Plásticas em Portugal*, Dissertação de mestrado em História Contemporânea apresentada á Faculdade de Letras da Universidade do Porto, no âmbito do seminário Património e Restauro, Volume I, 2001, Porto, .111-122;

[xxv] Francisco martins SARMENTO, *Expedição Científica á Serra da Estrela 1881*, Lisboa, Imprensa Nacional, 1883.

[xxvi] Portaria ao Governador Civil de Lisboa, proibindo que se lavrem as banquetas e terenos marginais dos rios, 29.07.1847; Portaria aos Governadores Civis do Porto , bragança, Vizeu e Guarda sobre a demolição de novos açudes feitos no Douro 14.10.1847 (3 anos depois de 1844, havia já novas construções mesmo de pois das campanhas de demolição); "Que nas terras que não têm actualmente nenhum areal ou acrescido se deve fazer (...)um tapume, e boleado ao menos de quinze braças de largura até à margem do rio, principalmente do sítio das Caneiras até às Ónias, aonde antigamente eram canaviaes, para defesa das terras, e que indevidamente foram roteadas", Portaria ao inspector geral das obras públicas do reino para mandar demolir os açudes, pesqueiras e nasceiros existentes no rio Douro" in *Legislação e Disposições Regulamentares* Sobre Rios, Valles, Açudes, Nasceiros, Pesqueiras, Pantanos e Barcas de Passagem coordenada, p.30-31 20.09.1852 [Ordinance of the minitry of Public Works Commerce and Industry 29 July, 1847 to the Civil Governor of Lisbon, banning the cultivation of banquettes and fields in the marginal rivers; Ordinance of the minitry of Public Works Commerce and Industry 12 April, 1847 to the Civil Governors of Porto, Bragança, Viseu and Guarda on the demolition of new dams made in the Douro (3 years after 1844, new buildings

covered with the bark of cork oak (Morais, 1988). In the summits of the hills in Viseu or in Alentejo fields used for pig breeding, had sheds (as late as the first half of the twentieth century) that could be made exclusively of plant material, fern or similar, canes and reed, sometimes walled or roofed with bark (Morais, 1988).

Thus, we can note that in a wide range of different landscapes the principles of creating even-temperature and humidity control conditions are the same. Abilities and technical skills to build structures that keep temperature and humidity stable were acquired empirically almost in every region of the country (Oliveira & Galhano, 1994). Before the use of electricity, the most efficient strategies to achieve insulation were: an outer covering with non-conducting materials; the absence of light; and the control of air circulation, for which stone and cork were, as today quite efficient. However, the insulating materials were also variable and distributed differently across the multiple landscapes.

In summary, at a local level, both temporary and lasting constructions for protection against extreme weather conditions were found in a wide variety of regions. Resources *a priori* regarded as of no economic value have been widely used across all the country, both in rich as well as in poor farming areas. Thus, in the Portuguese mosaic of the dry lands in the mountaintops, or in the savannah of Alentejo province the materials used for any kind of buildings or shelters seeking to minimise temperature extremes had an unexpressed economic value. This would be of equal importance to that observed for sand, trees, earth and stones used to defend riverbanks.

Therefore, in the nineteenth century, an era of water-related disasters, it was not only local strategies for protection against flooding and drought which were revealed as quite widespread but arid landscapes also started to become economic resources. They could supply building materials such as clay, sand and stone. In this context, even plants viewed as weeds in mainstream agricultural thinking could be shown to be of importance for use as insulation materials.

---

were built even after the effective campaigns of demolishing); "That the lands that currently do not have any sand or the increase is due to (...) a hoarding, and fillet at least fifteen fathoms wide and up the river, particularly the site of Caneiras until Onias, where formerly reed fields used to defend the land, and had been improperly routed", in 20.09.1852, Ordinance to the General Inspector of the Public Works of the kingdom, to send demolish the dams, fishing ponds nad nurserires existing the river Douro " Legislação e Disposições Regulamentares Sobre Rios, Valles, Açudes, Nasceiros, Pesqueiras, Pantanos e Barcas de Passagem coordenada, 30-31.

In response to the intensity of extreme weather phenomena, the human reaction to natural hazards revealed a much wider social and economic value for natural resources, which were crucial at a local level for material protection. Then, in the catastrophic flooding era of the 1800s these marginal resources might have acquired, economic significance, beyond the mere level of subsistence usage. Paradoxically, in the second half of the 1800s, with the golden age of *civil engineering taking off* (Diogo, 2000; Macedo, 2012), the protection of populations and landscapes against extreme weather conditions, erosion and destruction, was left to local endeavour as well as to local, non-scientific knowledge. Executive and legislative power had disregarded this state of affairs, which, would eventually become, although weakly represented in industry in the last quarter of the nineteen century, as in the first half of the twentieth century a profitable niche of the extractive industries (Rosas, 1994a; Lains, 2002; Guimarães, 2006).

Conclusions

One of the consequences of extreme weather occurrences from the 1850s onwards was the transformation of un-farmable landscapes with natural resources of low monetary value, into areas with resources of economic interest. Thus, one can conclude that, in the second half of the 1800s in Portugal, increased problems from water created issues. These were on the one hand, an unusual need for the consumption of low-value materials which then developed into a regular extraction of those goods for protecting the landscape. On the other hand, it helped to launch a new market for resources from areas of wastelands, meaning non-farming lands, which represented a far more intense use and level of economic activity beyond the *mere* level of subsistence (Clément, 2008; Melo, 2013). Eventually low-value resources with insulating properties as much as for their building characteristics were becoming valuable goods, apparently, as never before although disregarded as such by economic, political and engineering experts.

Thus, the problem of protection from extreme weather conditions provides a new perspective to the discussion around communal and public property. This brings a different approach to the one concerning the privatisation of communal areas for cattle grazing. The public response to the impact of overwhelming rainfall in inland areas, in the uplands and in the flood plains was delayed for far too long and consistently occurred after the devastation of huge areas of farmed land, caused by torrential rains, flash floods or hailstorms. The help provided to people and cattle proved to be, often inadequate for the magnitude of the events, allegedly provoked by these unexpected weather occurrences. It seems that politicians frequently under-estimated the claims and needs of communities in the aftermath of heavy rains or prolonged drought.

Unlike the political class living in Lisbon, local populations could not have afforded to wait with such a long delay of four years or more, just for the first attempt to design a legal framework for the public building of water-management systems. Communities living in a wide variety of landscapes were forced to deal alone with the unpredictability of the weather, in their daily lives. Moreover, when examination of rainfall data demonstrates that for almost three decades between the 1850s and 1880s, the country was squeezed between torrential flooding, from the mountains towards the shores, or from sea inundations inland, locals defended themselves with their already acquired secular knowledge. For many centuries, they had been adjusting to irregularities in the weather across a country rich in many microclimates. Somehow they seemed better prepared to face irregularities in the weather compared to the educated elite in the parliament, although they were not at all prepared to prevent diseases through proper sanitary procedures.

Thus, it can be shown that economic as well as social changes have been if not caused by at least triggered by environmental factors. Historiography about territorial management and environmental concerns within the nineteenth-century Europe, might start to examine how weather patterns or in some cases climate changes can be correlated with new activities structured around low-value materials and natural resources of disregarded landscapes. It can also view wastelands and low-value resources with a different insight today, far outside the usual paradigm of industrial and agricultural revolutions. Insight gained from the publication of the seminal book *Governing the Commons* by Elinor Ottrom, and works on climate data, has proved to be an adequate framework for such research.

References

Alarcão, D.J. De (1865) *Revista Agronómica*. Terceira série, Tomo III, 224.

Alarcão, M. De (1864) *Revista Agronómica*. Terceira série, Tomo II, 310.

Almeida, J.V. De (1899) "A Febre dos caminhos e ferro tem-nos distrahido a atenção d'outras obras importantes". Chronica agrícola. *Agricultura Contemporânea. Revista Agricola e Agronomica*, **37**, 37-40.

Almeida, M.A.P. de (2013) *Saúde Pública e Higiene na Imprensa Diária em Anos de Epidemias, 1854-1918*. Lisboa, Edições Colibri.

Anon. (1844) Requerimento da Baroneza de Alvaiázere Contra o Procedimento do Administrador do Concelho de Santarém por ter Demolido as Árvores que Protegiam as suas Propriedades nos Mouxões do Tejo. *Diário do Governo*, 20 de Maio, **118**, 1844.

Anon. (1865) Relatório da Direcção Geral dos Trabalhos Geodésicos, Chorográficos, Hydrográficos e Geológicos do Reino no Anno de 1863-1864. *Boletim do Ministério das Obras Públicas Commércio e Indústria*. **8**, Agosto, 166-175.

Anon. (1865) Um velho proprietário e pequeno Lavrador. "Comunicado". *Archivo Rural, Jornal de Agricultura, Artes e Sciências Correlativas*, **vol. VII**, 1865, 636-638.

Anon. (1871) Trabalhos Geodésicos, Topográphicos, Hydrográphicos, e Geológicos do Reino, Executados Desde 1 de Julho de 1868 a Dezembro de 1869. *Revista das Obras Públicas e Minas,* Tomo II, **23**, Novembro, 385-411.

Anon. (1877) *Annaes do Observatório do Infante D. Luís. Resumo das Principais Observações Meteorológicas Executadas Durante o Período de 20 Annos Decorridos Desde 1856-1875*. Lisboa, Imprensa Nacional.

Baldwin, P. (1999) *Contagion and the State in Europe, 1830-1930*. Cambridge, Cambridge University Press.

Barca, S. (2007) Enclosing the River: Industrialization and the Property Rights Discourse in the Liri Valle (South of Italy), 1806–1916. *Environment and History*, **13**, 3–23.

Bevilacqua, P. and Corona, G. (2000) *Ambiente e Risorse nel Mezzogiorno Contemporaneo*. Roma, Meridiana Libri.

Branco, R.M.C. (2005) *The Cornerstones of Modern Government: Maps, Weights and Measures and Census in Liberal Portugal (19th century)*, Thesis Submitted assessment with a view obtaining the degree of Doctor in History and Civilization from the European University Institute, Florence, August.

Brantz, D. (2011) 'Risky Business': Disease, Disaster and the Unintended Consequencesof Epizootics in Eighteenth- and Nineteenth-Century France and Germany. *Environment and History,* **17**, 35–51.

Brito, R.S. (1960) *Palheiros de Mira, Formação e Declínio de um Aglomerado de Pescadores*. Lisboa.

Capello, H, and Torres, L. (1883) Viagem à Serra do Gerez e suas Caldas em Setembro de 1882. *Boletim da Sociedade de Geografia de Lisboa*, 4ª série, Nº 6, Lisboa, **533, 541,** 526-542.

Cascão, R. (1993) *Demografia e sociedade*. In: *História de Portugal*. Dir. José Mattoso, **vol. V**, Lisboa, Editorial Estampa, 425-439.

Clément, V. (2008) Spanish Wood Pasture: Origin and Durability of an Historical Wooded Landscape in Mediterranean Europe. *Environment and History*, **14**, 67–87.

Delgado, C. and Folque, F. (1868) *Relatório da Arborização Geral do País*. Lisboa, Imprensa Nacional.

Diogo, M. P. (1994) *A Construção de uma Identidade Profissional* Tese de Doutoramento em História e Filosofia das Ciências (especialidade de Epistemologia),Universidade Nova de Lisboa, Lisboa.

Eça, B. F., de A. d' (1866) *Memoria Acerca das Irrigações na França,Itália, Bélgica e Hespanha por Bento Fortunato de Moura Coutinho de Almeida d'Eça Capitão Graduado do Corpo de Engenharia Militar e Engenheiro Chefe da Segunda Classe do Corpo de Engenharia Civil*. Lisboa, Imprensa Nacional.

Ferreira, D. de B. (2006) *As Características do Clima Actual*. In: *Geografia de Portugal*, **Vol. I**, Coordenação Medeiros, C. A. De, Lisboa, Círculo de Leitores, 332-370.

Ficalho, C. de, (1867-1868) Conferência feita pelo Exmo sr. Conde de Ficalho, Director do Instituto Geral de Agricultura e Professor da Escola Politécnica de Lisboa. *Revista Agrícola,* Tomo **V**, 3ª série, 5-8.

Folque, F. (1872) Trabalhos Geodésicos, Topográphicos e Geológicos do Reino. *Revista de Obras Públicas e Minas,* Tomo II, **23**, 386-411.

Graça, M.V. (1871) Relatório Geral dos Trabalhos Executados na Direcção das Obras Públicas do Districto de Évora. *Revista de Obras Públicas e Minas*, ano II, Lisboa, **225**, 225-230.

Guimarães, P.E. (2001) *Indústria e Conflito no meio Rural, os Mineiros Alentejanos (1858-1938)*. Lisboa, Edições Colibri e CIDEHUS.

Guimarães, P.E. (2006) *Elites e Indústria no Alentejo (1890-1960).* Edições Colibri-CIDEUS-UE, Lisboa, 289-303.

Hall, M. (2005) *Earth Repair: George Perkins Marsh and the Restoration Tradition.* Charlesville, University of Virginia Press.

Hobsbawm, E. (1975) *The Age of Capital 1848-1875.* London, Weidenfeld and Nicolson.

Horta, T. da P. e, (1861) Diário da Câmara dos Deputados, 01.02.1861. *Diário de Lisboa*, Fevereiro, p. 280.

Laíns, P. and Silva, A.F. da (2005) *História Económica de Portugal* O século XX, **Vol. III**, Lisboa, Imprensa de Ciências Sociais.

Lamb, H.H. (1982) *Climate, History, and the Modern World*. London;

Leite, A. (1999) *As Pesqueiras do Rio Minho. Economia, Sociedade e Património* Caminha, Corema-Associação de defesa do Património.

Loureiro, A. (1875) Memória do Mondego e da Barra da Figueira. III. Descripção dosprojectos de Obras para o Melhoramento do Porto e Barra da Figueira, e do Rio Mondego e Campos de Coimbra. *Revista de Obras Públicas e Minas,* Tomo IV, **62**, Lisboa, **57-58, 61-66**, 53- 94.

Loureiro, A. (1880) Memoria Sobre o Melhoramento do Mondego entre Coimbra e Foz do Dão. *Revista de Obras Públicas e Minas*. Tomo XI, Lisboa, **75**, 61-99.

Macedo, M. (2012) *Projetar e Construir a Nação. Engenheiros, Ciência e Território em Portugal no séc. XIX*. Lisboa: Instituto de Ciências Sociais.

Magalhães, J.M. De (1862) Relatório Apresentado a Sua Exca. O sr. Ministro das Obras Públicas. *Boletim do Ministério das Obras Públicas Commércio e Indústria,* **5**.

Magalhães, J.M. De (1862) Relatório Apresentado a Sua Exca. O sr. Ministro das Obras Públicas. *Boletim do Ministério das Obras Públicas Commércio e Indústria*, **11**.

Magalhães, J.M. De (1864) Relatório apresentado a Sua Exca. O sr.Ministro das ObrasPúblicas, pelo Engenheiro Florestal João Maria de Magalhães, Alferes do Exército. *Boletim do Ministério das Obras Públicas Commércio e Indústria,* **12**.

Melo, C. J. De (2010) *Contra Cheias e Tempestades: Consciência do Território, políticas de Águas e Florestas no século XIX em Portugal 1851-1886*. Thesis submitted for the degree of Doctor in History and Civilization from the European University Institute, Florence, November 2010.

Melo, C. J. De (2011) Breaking the whiteness in the Alpine landscape: An heritage from the nation-states building process. In: *Environmental Law and Mountains: Lessons from European Ranges*. Supervised by Marco Onida, ed. Patrícia Quilacq, Insbruck, European Alps Convention, 10-21.

Melo, C. J. De, (2013) A questão fácil dos baldios: não lhes tocar. *Debates. I Encontro Internacional de História Ambiental Lusófona*, no.1, 2013,Coimbra, CES Contexto, 21-68. http://www.ces.uc.pt/publicacoes/cescontexto/ficheiros/cescontexto_debates_i.pdf

Mendía, H. De (1880), Algumas verdades sobre administração florestal. *Gazeta dos Lavradores*, 152-55.

Miquel, P. 1998 [1992] *Le Seconde Empire*. Perrim, Paris.

Morais, J.A.D. de (1988) A Transumância dos Gados Serranos e o Alentejo. *Novos Estudos Eborenses,* nº 3, Évora, Câmara Municipal de Évora.

Nobre, J. A., (2001) *Património Rural na Terra de Miranda e Artes Plásticas em Portugal.* Dissertação de Mestrado em História Contemporânea apresentada à Faculdade de Letras da Universidade do Porto, no âmbito do seminário Património e Restauro, Volume I, Porto, 111-122.

Oliveira, E. V. de, Galhano, F. *et al*. (1994) *Construções Primitivas em Portugal.* 3rd ed [1st ed, 1969], Lisboa.

Oliveira, F. de P. C. e (1867) *Informações Para a Estatística Industrial Publicadas Pela Repartição de Pesos e Medidas. Districto de Aveiro*, Lisboa, Imprensa Nacional.

Ostrom, E. (1990) *Governing the Commons: The Evolution of Institutions for CollectiveAction*. Cambridge, Cambridge University Press.

Pery, G.A. (1875) Geographia Estatistica Geral de Portugal e Colónias, 1ª ed., Lisboa, Imprensa Nacional.

Pfister, C. (1984) *Das Klima der Schweiz von 1525-1860 und seine Bedeutung in der Geschichte vonBevölkerung und Landwirtschaft / Christian Pfister Band 1 Klimageschichte der Schweiz 1525-1860. Bern*, Stuttgart: Paul Haupt.

Pfister, C. (2002) Strategian Zur Bewaltigung von Naturkatastrophen seit *1500* in *Am Tag Danach –Zur Bewaltigung von NaturKatastrophen in der Schweiz1500-2000*, Haupt, Bern, 209-255.

Rackham, O. and Grove, A. T. (2001) *The Nature of Mediterranean Europe. An Ecological History*. New Haven and London, Yale University Press.

Ribeiro, J. S. (1854) Resolução XII. In: *Obras nos Rios e Junto a Pontes in Resoluções do Conselho de Estado. Tomo I na secção do Contencioso Administrativo Coligidas e explicadas por José Silvestre Ribeiro*, Lisboa, Imprensa Nacional, 60-194.

Ribeiro, O. and Lautensach, H. (1987) *Geografia de Portugal: A Posição Geográfica e o Território*. (actualização e comentários de Suzanne Daveau), Tomo I, Lisboa, Edições João Sá da Costa.

Rodrigues, M. (2007) *Empresas e empresários das indústrias transformadoras, na sub-região da Ria de Aveiro, 1864-1931*. Lisboa, Fundação Calouste Gulbenkian.

Rosas, F. (1994a) "O Estado Novo nos anos 30". In: *História de Portugal*, vol 7, Lisboa, Círculo de Leitores, 243-268.

Rosas, F. (1994b) "Economia de guerra e política económica de guerra" In: *História de Portugal*, vol. 7, Lisboa, Círculo de Leitores, 322-353.

Rotherham, I.D. (2010) *Yorkshire's Forgotten Fenlands*. Barnsley, Wharncliffe Publishing.

Rotherham, I.D., Agnoletti, M. and Handley, C. (2010) Cultural Severance and the End of Tradition. *Landscape Archaeology and Ecology*, **8** (1 &2).

Saavedra, M.A. de A.M. (2010) *Uma Questão Nacional" Enredos da malária em Portugal, séculos XIX e XX*. Doutoramento em Ciências Sociais -Especialidade: Antropologia Social e Cultural , Lisboa, ICS-UL.

Sarmento, F.M. (1883) *Expedição Científica á Serra da Estrela 1881*. Lisboa, Imprensa Nacional.

Smith, A.K. (2005) *Public Works in an Autocratic State: Water Sulies in an Imperial Russian Town. Environment and History*, **1**, 319–42.

Smout, T. C. (2000) *Nature Contested: Environmental History in Scotland and Northern England Since 1600*. Edinburgh, Edinburgh University Press.

Soares, R. de M. (1863-64) Chronica Agrícola. *Archivo Rural, Jornal de Agricultura, Artes e Sciências Correlativas*, **vol. VI**, 1863-64, 638.

Soares, R. de M. (1865) Um velho proprietário e pequeno Lavrador, Comunicado. *Archivo Rural, Jornal de Agricultura, Artes e Sciências Correlativas*, **vol. VII**, 636-638

Soares, R. de M. (1865-66) Chrónica Agrícola. *Archivo Rural, Jornal de Agricultura, Artes e Sciências Correlativas*, **vol. VIII**, 359.

Soares, R. de M. (1867) Chronica Agrícola. *Archivo Rural, Jornal de Agricultura, Artes e Sciências Correlativas*, **vol. IX**, 135.

Soares, R. de M. (1868) Chronica Agrícola. *Archivo Rural, Jornal de Agricultura, Artes e Sciências Correlativas*, **Vol. X**.

Taylor, A.J.P. (1984) *The Struggle for Mastery in Europe, 1848-1918*. Oxford, Oxford University Press.

Temple, S. (2011) Forestation and its Discontents: The Invention of an Uncertain Landscape in Southwestern France, 1850–Present. *Environment and History*, **17**, 13–34.

Valladas, M. R. (1862) Oficio e Relatório Acerca do Resultado do Primeiro Ensaio de Drainagem pelo Engenheiro Adido à Repartição de Agricultura. *Boletim do Ministério das Obras Públicas Comércio e Indústria*, **4,** 290- 295.

Valladas, M. R. (1864), Trabalhos Para Enxugo d'um Paul em Lagos. *Archivo Rural, Jornal de Agricultura, Artes e Sciências Correlativas*, v**ol. VII**, 145-149.

Valladas, M. R. (1875) Memória Sobre o reconhecimento dos Rios, Ribeiras, Barras e Terrenos Marginaes no Litoral a Partir de Villa Real de Santo António, na Foz do Guadiana, até à Ribeira de Melides, Proximo à Foz do Sado. *Revista de Obras Públicas e Minas,* Tomo VI, **72**, 480-483, 453-489.

Vivier, N. (2002) *The Management and use of Commons in France in the Eighteenth and Nineteenth Centuries*. In: *The Management of Common Land in North West Europe, c. 1500-1850* CORN – Comparative Rural History of North Sea Area, vol. 8, Turnhout, Brepols, 143-173.

Warde, P. (2002) "Common rights and common lnads in south west Germany" In: *The Management of Common Land in Northwest Europe, c. 1500-1850*CORN –Comparative Rural History of North Sea Area, vol. 8, Turnhout, Brepols, 195-224.

Zagli, A., (2001) *Il lago e la Comunità. Storia di Bientina un «castello» di pescatori nella Toscana Moderna*, Firenze, Edizioni Polistampa.

Houses of God: the cult of the Saints and protection against natural threats in late medieval Portugal

Pedro Picoito

Instituto de Estudos Medievais [Institute for Medieval Studies] Faculdade de Ciências Sociais e Humanas, Universidade NOVA de Lisboa

Abstract

In the Middle Ages the supernatural invocation against natural threats consisted of two main forms. Firstly, cyclical rites – processionals that at the annual solstices or at other especially significant times marking the transition through the solar calendar, moved the faithful to make a pilgrimage to a sanctuary or to the border of a local place. Here the faithful would pray, make offerings, pay indulgences or take part in festivities. Secondly, piacular rites – extraordinary requests for help made to saints, icons or relics, by means of processions or prayers. Here the faithful would ask them to intervene to alleviate unexpected natural calamities.

This chapter will study types of invocation to saints for protection against environmental threats, with a focus on the period between the fourteenth and the sixteenth centuries in Portugal. The analysis is based on selected case studies providing insight into the long cultural struggle between the Church and popular cults for the symbolic domination of such forms of invocation.

Key words: Cult of the saints; popular religion; fertility rites; rogations; pilgrimages.

"Levanto os braços aos céus	*"I raise my arms to the skies*
Aqui – mulher, terra, mar –	*Here – woman, land, sea –*
Aqui só pode ser a casa de Deus"	*Only here can the house of God be"*
	Ruy Belo

Introduction

In the modern West, characterised both by the influence of religion and dependency on the environment, invoking supernatural powers is the main way of trying to minimize the effects of the elements. This is so prevalent that several historiographical paradigms of the modern age, for example Max Weber's famous quote of "the disenchantment of the world", relates technical and scientific progress to the decline of religious beliefs and practices (1904-1905; Boudon, 2001). For centuries however, Christianity proceeded towards another "disenchantment of the world," trying to dominate nature's mysterious forces. This was especially at moments when these forces fell drastically upon humans, either in places where the natural forces were most powerful and impressive (on the sea, by waterfalls, lakes, mountains and forests); or during the annual cycle of life with domination over the symbols of the new cosmic order starting with the Incarnation of Christ. This is the cult of the saints and the liturgical calendar (Brown, 1980; Vauchez, 1988a; Muir, 1997, 55-80; Markus, 1998, 85-136; Howard-Johnston & Hayward, 1999; Boesch-Gajano, 1999; Vauchez, 2003, 255-264; Benvenuti *et al.*, 2005; Baschet, 2006, 65-78; Briggs, 2011, 204-211). Alongside this history, the Christianisation of Europe is also the Christianisation of European space and time.

On the whole, in the Christian tradition, turning to the supernatural for protection against storms, epidemics or the dangers that threaten daily life is associated with specific saints. Some of the main ones are St Barbara (storms and fires), St Nicolas (sea travel), St Christopher (travel on land and river crossings), St Isidore (harvests), St Peter (fishing), St. Anton (stockbreeding), St. Margaret (childbirth), St. Sebastian (plague), St. Lazarus (leprosy), St Roch (skin diseases), St Blaise (throat diseases), St Lucia (eye diseases), and St Apollonia (toothaches) (Duchet-Suchaux & Pastoureau, 1994; Farmer, 2003). The devotions for these saints are common across Christianity, but there are also locally venerated saints that take the functions attributed to the universal saints. In Portugal for instance, there is the case of the famous St Anthony, whose cult sometimes replaces the one of St Peter amongst fishermen, or of Our Lady, the universal intercessor in various situations.

Apart from the dedication of churches to one or several patron saints, in the Middle Ages the supernatural invocation against natural threats consisted of two main forms. First, cyclical rites – processionals which at the annual solstices or other especially significant times marking the passage through the solar calendar, moved the faithful to make a pilgrimage to a sanctuary or to the borders of a local place to pray, make offerings, pay indulgences or take part in festivities. Secondly, and using Durkheim's concepts, piacular rites – extraordinary requests for help made to saints, icons or relics, by means of processions or prayers, asking them to ameliorate unexpected natural disasters. Piacular rites often gave rise to celebration rites in the form of annual pilgrimages to churches consecrated to the mediating saint.

These two sets of rites are not defined as being opposed to each other or mutually exclusive. On the contrary, they interpenetrate and interpolate each other into a system of ritual practices that historians call, not without controversy, popular religion (Van Engen, 1983, 519-522; Lauwers, 1987; Schmitt, 1988a, 1-27; Schmitt, 2001, 9-12; Duffy, 2005, XV-XXVIII; Shinners, 2009, XVII-XXI). The categorisation presented here is only a provisional, flexible and outline conceptual framework. Cyclical rites often start as piacular rites and these tend to assume celebratory cyclical forms. In the rest of this chapter, I set out an approach to these two forms of piety in Portugal between the fourteenth and sixteenth centuries. As it is impossible to analyse thoroughly such an extensive geographic area and chronological period, I will firstly try to obtain a generic perspective from selected case studies.

Cyclical and solstice rites

Medieval cyclical rites focus very frequently on the fertility of the fields and livestock, of which collective survival depends. Jean-Claude Schmitt reminds us that, "in a society of destitution, the anxiety of material abundance plays a big role in popular rituals" (Schmitt, 1988b). Durkheim had already noted that this very concern seems to dominate primitive religious cults (1912). As an echo of very ancient ceremonies that enhance nature these rites are focused mainly between the spring and autumn equinoxes, the time of germination and harvest (Espírito Santo, 1990). In the liturgical calendar, it is the time from Carnival, at the beginning of the Easter cycle with a celebration of excesses, which already announces the spring revival, until All Souls Day on November 2nd. This is a celebration of the dead and the symbolic beginning of autumn. The high point of this calendar is the festival of St John on June 24th, corresponding to the summer solstice (Baschet, 2006).

The most characteristic agrarian rituals of the medieval West were spring rogations or litanies, ancient processions destined to ensure the success of the harvests. In the canonical form prescribed by the Church these occurred twice a year: lesser rogations on the day of St Marcus (April 25th in the calendar of the Latin Church), and greater rogations on the three days before Ascension Day, marking the end of Easter time (Shinners, 2009, 297-302). Rogations, however, eventually became the archetype of all Christian rites protecting against disease or bad weather, as Edward Muir highlights (1997, 67). André Vauchez identifies the liturgical birth of these ceremonies in the fifth century in Gaul and its dissemination throughout the whole Franc territory from the Council of Orléans in 511. In the eleventh century, the Roman liturgy would adopt these ceremonies as three-day processions *pro diversis calamitatibus* occurring before the celebration of Ascension to pray for averting disasters that expressly included attacks from wild animals, epidemics and storms (1988b). Emmanuel Le Roy Ladurie is surprised with the "discretion" of such practices in Montaillou in the first quarter of the fourteenth century, so much so that rogations had been compulsory from the previous century in the dioceses of Occitania (1982, 465-466). Similarly, Portuguese medieval sources provide little information in this respect and perhaps that is why the history of rogations in Portugal is still to be written.

In *Legenda Aurea*, Iacopo de Varezze gives us a complete description of what the ritual and the sense of rogations would have been in the second half of the thirteenth century. The name *rogation* "*means prayer, plea, request*" because "*during those days we implore the help of the saints*". The high moment of the rite was the procession, which went round the borders of the parish, followed by mass to attract divine favour on the land and harvests, and symbolically to take ownership of the community space. During the procession "*one takes a cross standing up high and bells are rung. In certain churches men drag a long-tailed dragon. One by one, all the saints are invoked for protection. The cross is taken and bells are rung to scare away the demons, because just as a king marches with his army parading the royal insignia, whether they be trumpets or banners, so Christ the eternal king marching with the militant Church has the bells as trumpets and the cross as a banner. And so like a tyrant feels fearful when listening to the trumpets and viewing the banners of a mighty enemy king on his territory, so the demons that roam in the dark are attacked by fear when they hear Christ's trumpets – the bells – and view the banner – the cross. This is why, so it is said, church bells are rung during storms, so that the demons that stir the air listen to Christ's trumpets and run away with fear, and the storm calms down. There is certainly another reason, which is to inform the faithful of the danger and incite them to pray for the storm to go away*" (Ryan, 1993, 285-289).

Although rogations have not always had the structure and elements described above, as they were often adapted to local circumstances, they became the universal model of propitiatory rites in the Middle Ages. This was mainly because they Christianised earlier traditions. Social control of such ceremonies and of many others, close to popular culture, received special attention from the Church over the centuries. Arising from the Christianisation of ancestral spring pagan festivities, such as the Roman Robigalia, rogations became the most important pastoral strategy to structure fertility rites under suspicion of heterodoxy (Christian, 1991, 143-149; Muir, 1997, 66-67; Duffy, 2005, 136-139, 279-280). Hence, the author of *Legenda Aurea*, a pious and learned bishop, manifested the scepticism typical of the ecclesiastic elites of his time, in respect of the popular view of a custom that was verging on magic. He states, ("*so it is said...*"), preferred to give it an allegorical and moral sense ("*warning the faithful about the danger and inciting them to pray*") (Schmitt, 2001, 77-96). An allegorical and moral sense is already present in the image of the dragon, a symbol of evil, included in the procession and opposed to the saints, symbols of good, invoked in the litany (Le Goff 1977; Baschet, 1999, 264).

In Portugal, just as in the whole of Europe, rogations are related to two folk festivities that survive to this day. Lesser rogations preceded the *Maias*, celebrated at the beginning of May "*with a sense of purification and exaltation of fertility and abundance via various actions of imitative, propitiatory or, more probably, prophylactic ritual magic*", according to ethnologist Ernesto Veiga de Oliveira (1995, 97-118). Greater rogations were associated with the so-called 'Day of the Wheat Ear' in which the faithful collected the first fruits of their harvests, symbolised in wheat and flower arrangements, and hung them at home for one year with "*an expressed idea of beneficial virtue*" over the results of their annual agricultural work. Ernesto Veiga de Oliveira points out the regional variations of the *Maias* celebration in Minho, Douro and Beira Litoral on the one hand, in Trás-os-Montes and Beira Interior on the other hand, as well as in Estremadura, Alentejo and the Algarve. He finishes by drawing comparisons between the Algarve *Maias* with the ones from Provence (France). It is curious to note this tripartite differentiation roughly coincides with the classic division of Portuguese geography into north Atlantic, north inland, and Mediterranean south proposed by Orlando Ribeiro (1945), a strong indication of its persistence in popular culture to this day.

An example of the vitality of the spring rites in Portugal, and of the ambiguity with which they were viewed by the authorities, is the famous example of the prohibition of the *Maias* in Lisbon in 1385. The king and the municipality forbade this custom in the capital city and tried to replace it with festivities that corresponded to the liturgical calendar. This was so that they could ask for Heavenly protection against the serious crisis that the kingdom was then undergoing, due to the dynastic interruption and the war with Castile (Ventura, 2003, 163-172), Approximately half a century later (Amado, 1993 a, b) the royal chronicler Fernão Lopes wrote the following in the *Crónica de D. João I*:
"*Seeing how for many years the people of the city had been admonished by preaching, started from some sins and damned customs of the gentiles, who used them for a long time, namely errors of idolatry for which, according to the Holy Scripture, God seriously torments the people (…) they will establish and order, promising God to keep forever and from then on, for themselves and for their successors, in the city and in its limits, not ever using spells, nor ties, nor callings of the devils, nor potions, nor work of dowser, nor masks, nor dreams, nor cast the wheel, nor cast lots, nor any other thing that the art of physics does not consent to, and also that they do not sing the* Janeiras, *nor the* Maias, *nor any other month of the year, nor steal waters, nor cast lots nor any other observance that belonged to such feats*" (Lopes de Almeida & Magalhães Basto, 1990, 101; Marques 1987, 171).

This text, that Ana Maria Rodrigues calls a "true catalogue" of heterodox practices (2000, 45), illustrates well the difficult relationship between agrarian rites and official religion (Beirante, 2011, 174). On the one hand, it shows that in the fourteenth and fifteenth centuries there was still a clear awareness of the pagan origin of these rites and their closeness to "*idolatry*" and the "*damned customs of the gentiles*". This might help explain the reference to the limits of the city, indicating the rural character that these rituals would have had and of the eternal distrust of peasant culture by civil and ecclesiastic authorities (Baschet, 2006, 310-314; Mattoso, 2009, 155-167). On the other hand, it also shows that these were practices that were strongly rooted amongst the population, as they "*used them for a long time*", despite the prolonged effort of the Church to eradicate them ("*for many years the people of the city had been admonished by preaching*"), and to eradicate the diversity of the divination and propitiatory rites which one can generically call magic, in which the practices were included. Lastly, one is explicitly told that the *Janeiras* and the *Maias* were sung, an element of collective celebration by sound, which is also present in the litanies for the saints and in rogations.

Indeed, this situation shows that the Church and the political powers try to reinforce the Christianisation of fertility rites of pagan origin with the festivities of the corresponding liturgical calendar. For example, the *Janeiras* were replaced by the festivity of the Circumcision of Jesus (January 1st), and the *Maias* were replaced both by the festivity of Our Lady of the Ladder (May 1st), which was a very popular festivity in Lisbon (Moita, 1927, 219; Santana & Sucena, 1994, 638). The same was the case with the festivity of the Holy Cross or celebration of the crosses, the common name for the festivity of the Invention of the Holy Cross (May 3rd) (Farmer, 2003, 118-119). Apparently, these replacements had little success, since the *Janeiras* and the *Maias* had to be condemned again by Archbishop João Anes between 1393 and 1402, and by his successor D. João Afonso Esteves de Azambuja at the 1403 synod (Garcia y Garcia, 1982, 334-335). It is indeed an old concern of the Church. In the Iberian West during the 6th century, St. Martin of Braga was already forbidding the faithful to celebrate the January calends, the first day of each year in the Roman calendar (Nascimento, 1997, 113, 121, 157). As Jean-Claude Schmitt reminds us, the cycles around the solstices and the equinoxes, especially the spring ones, were always moments of strong confrontation between the clerical culture and folk culture for the symbolic domination of the calendar (Schmitt, 2001, 175-177). If the Church was trying to Christianise space with the procession, it was also trying to Christianise time with the celebration.

Nevertheless, the control of space and of the material forms of cult was as important to the Church as was the domination of time. Nothing is said about this in the case of Lisbon, but we know that in 1477 the diocese of Braga forbade the custom of celebrating "*masses on the fields and near trees and in other dishonest places, places of great danger because of the rains, winds and storms and other inconveniences that many times occur*" (Garcia y Garcia, 1982, 117). Masses associated with rogations (or "*clamours*" as the synod calls them) were only authorised in ecclesiastic spaces. The diocese imposed a prohibition on other celebrations, showing once again the relationship between this liturgy and what was considered noise. They were also suspicious of paganism, that constant topic of the medieval discourse about superstitions: "*And if it happens that some processions or clamours are to be made, we defend and order that those processions or clamours do not go to the hills nor to similar places but go to churches and monasteries and sanctuaries, i.e. places for prayer, and that there they clamour and pray to God and listen to mass, because the rest is more a work of gentiles than of Christians.*" Almost a thousand years after St Martin's admonitions against the cult of fauns and nymphs, the Church of Braga was still associating the open air liturgy with a pagan survival. This was a sign that outside the churches, space continued to be disputed between the orthodoxy and popular religion.

Commemorative and piacular rites

The annual festivities of the saints which one can define by adapting Durkheim's concept as "representative or commemorative rites" that "serve to morally rebuild individuals and groups" (1912) are also cyclical devotions in the medieval and modern West. Cities, villages, brotherhoods or individuals honour their protectors in this way with pilgrimages. Usually, these were associated with the agricultural calendar (Muir, 1997, 55-72; Schmitt, 2004, 204-213; Beirante, 2011, 173-184; Coelho, 2011, 144-169). Sometimes these festivities are also a memory of the collective response to any extraordinary and unexpected event, especially storms, epidemics or other natural disasters. These drive people to build a temple (church) in honour of a saint or devote an annual procession to this saint. William Christian, who studied the phenomenon in modern Spain, compares these collective vows to "corporately contracted debt or the interests on a perpetual loan". The regular payment was the reason for prayer so that the original calamity would not be repeated in the future, "and that way ceremonies in a time of crisis tended to become rites of annual celebration, not very different from rogations prescribed by the liturgical calendar" (Christian, 1991, 144). This characteristic brings them closer to "piacular rites", a name given by Durkheim to the "sad celebrations whose object is to face a calamity or simply to remember it and lament it" (1912).

Despite being a ritual of unity and collective identity in the image of spring rogations (Duffy, 2005, 136-137), pilgrimages were not always exempt from creating conflict between the Church and the local population. An example of the difficult balance between ecclesiastic and popular readings of the same rite is the so-called "devotion of the naked", a piacular cult started in the fifteenth century and studied by Luís Krus (2011, 133-149). It is known that until the twentieth century farmers around Coimbra rang a bell while going through their cultivated fields. A custom which tradition associated with the cult of the Martyrs from Morocco, in which five Franciscans were killed in 1220 in North Africa. Their relics were preserved in the monastery of Santa Cruz [in Coimbra]. This custom, which is clearly very similar to rogations by the use of bells, could occur at any time of the year. However, its origin goes back to the "procession of the naked" in which barefoot men, naked from the waist up, would walk the distance between the monastery of St. Francis, on the left bank of the Mondego river, and the monastery of Santa Cruz, on the right bank, on the morning of January 16th (festivity of the Martyrs of Morocco). The annual procession would fulfil a vow made in 1423 by the inhabitants of the neighbouring village of S. Martinho do Bispo at the time of a virulent plague. The Martyrs of Morocco were invoked both against the plague and for protection of the fields but their festival occurred in winter and not in spring. This shows the referred influence of spring rogations on other ceremonies performed against natural threats. The "devotion of the naked", very much associated with the rural population, was forbidden in 1641, authorised again a few years later and permanently forbidden in 1798 with indecencies and noise given as reasons (Marques 1987, 164-165). Once again, the control over forms of ritual within the cult, including sound, proved to be central in the negotiation between civil and ecclesiastic powers and popular religion.

It is no wonder the strategy to circumscribe the cults to forms that could be controlled by the clergy was so important, to the point that sometimes rogations or pilgrimages gave privilege to the space occupied by the churches themselves, as shown by the previously quoted synod of Braga in 1477. This is not the only case. Friar Agostinho de Santa Maria, in *Santuário Mariano* – a work of the first quarter of the eighteenth century that gathers various reports on the origins of sanctuaries and pilgrimages all over the country – relates that in May 1372 Évora was devasted by "*a sudden storm, so rainy and unbearable due to continuous rains, that persevered for several days and ravaged all cultivated fields, and the poor farmers were without any hope of being able to collect any of the wheat grains"*

(Santa Maria, 1716, 7-9). In order to deflect the "punishment from Heaven", the bishop, D. Martinho Gil de Brito, then ordered "*a procession of prayers so that the Lady would beg from her most clement Son the preservation of the fruits, which were seen as completely lost*". The procession began with a solemn mass at the main cathedral, gathering the clergy and the people of the town, and during the homily "*the audience began to be moved by true contrition and penance. The sermon had not yet been finished when it stopped raining and the air was appeased, upon which everyone rendered their grace to God, singing loudly and with great joy hymns and songs of praise to the pious Queen of Angels, who had achieved serenity for them; and it was then that the procession went out and came back with the sun*". By order of bishop D. Martinho, the chapter and the senate then made the vow of carrying out a "*general procession*" every year to give thanks, "*and they persevered in it up to the present time*" adds Friar Agostinho de Santa Maria.

Friar Agostinho quotes several earlier authors as sources of the miracle, amongst which was the sixteenth-century author André de Resende. We do not know if the first reports, lost today, were similar or whether they were altered. Anyway, it is worth noting two characteristics that reveal the Church's care in ensuring the orthodoxy of this cult.

First, the miracle occurs during a mass service inside the cathedral, in a space and time completely controlled by the bishop, who calls the people to the ceremony and who then celebrates it. After the miracle, hymns and liturgical chants are sung. This shows the difference between the orthodox sacralisation of sound and the suspicious so-called noise and "clamours" which were being associated with the rogations by the synod of Braga in 1477 and by the authorities who forbade the "procession of the naked" in Coimbra. Only then does the procession come outdoors, where the risk of escaping the ecclesiastic structure is greater. Likewise, the vow of celebrating mass and the annual procession are enacted by the chapter and the senate, the two highest collective powers of the town. This symbolizes the diocese and the council, and summing up the urban community. If it is a specific bishop that originates the festivity, it is the whole town that ensures its future, as the survival of the protecting festivity represents the survival of the protected community.
Secondly, the report does not attribute a demonic origin to bad weather, unlike the deep-rooted popular belief, but moralises it as a punishment from Heaven. As in *Legenda Aurea*, half a millennium before, Friar Agostinho de Santa Maria sees the cause of the miracle in penance and not in magic. Natural disasters demanded conversion and not superstition.

This aspect is very significant because folklore does not easily distinguish one aspect from another. The distance between cult and magic is short and passes, before anything else, through the minds and hearts of humans. As Marcel Mauss insists, the difference between magic and religious rites is not in the form "but in the conditions in which they are produced and mark the place they occupy in the set of social practises" (1903). Hence he defined the magic rite as "any rite that is not part of an organised cult, a private, secret, mysterious rite, tending at the limit toward the forbidden rite", which reiterates the distinction made by Durkheim, for whom the profanation of sacred things and the absence of a centralised structure are part of the very notion of magic (1912). Liturgical spaces, times, rites and objects were often used, on the margins of the Church, for devotional purposes and senses. The Church looked at them with distrust and tried to control them, not always with success (Shinners, 2009, 475-485). It was a cultural war which started much earlier and which manifests itself in the eternal conflict between erudite and popular culture in the religious field (Kieckeffer, 1996; Schmitt, 2001, 42-52).

This case shows, therefore, the circumstances of a festivity under the eyes of the ecclesiastic hierarchy. Outside the more solemn sacred space, when occurring on the streets, churchyards or in suburban chapels, the leading role was transferred to council authorities or to local or professional brotherhoods. The festivities of the saints were also, and especially, civic, corporate and ethnic devotions, associating a cult with an urban community, a trade or a minority.

The establishment of the chapels of St Blaise and St Sebastian in Évora in the fifteenth century may be compared to the previous case. When referring to the chapel of the Roman martyr outside the city walls, Manuel Fialho and Francisco Fonseca explain in the eighteenth century "*that the people of Évora raised the chapel following a vow made to the saint to be free from the 1479 plague, taking the saint as an advocate together with St Blaise, and so they built the two churches in 1482*" (Fialho & Fonseca, 1728, 401). This vow has been "*religiously observed*" since then with a procession at the time of the respective festivities, that is January 20th for St Sebastian and February 3rd for St Blaise. In the case of St Blaise it is explicitly indicated that "*on the day of the saint the chapter and the senate will go to the festivity in a procession*". Although in Portugal, both saints are traditional intercessors against the plague, the episode justifies the civic cult by which "*the people of Évora*" are collectively made responsible, and not only the ecclesiastic cult.

According to André Vauchez, the civic cult is the joint set of religious manifestations "*in which the civil power has a determining role, especially through the action of local and municipal authorities*" (2003, 247). Civic cults are frequently born or maintained through the council's power and initiative, although under the watchful eye of the Church. The generalised favour they find amongst the population converts them into ceremonies of legitimisation and political representation in urban societies (Muir 1997, 232-239; Gouveia, 2001). Note that, in Alentejo, chapels devoted to St Sebastian, St Blaise and other intercessors against the plague are generally located outside the settlements and along external route-ways in order to guarantee supernatural protection against the entry of epidemics (Vieira da Silva, 2002-2006, 294). This is the case in Évora, where the chapels of St. Sebastian and St. Blaise are located near the roads that lead to the nearest towns, respectively Lisbon to the west and Beja to the south (Beirante, 1995; Daveau, 1998, 104-105, 122-123; Simplício, 2002-2006; Bilou, 2005; Beirante, 2007, 193-200). The location turns the pilgrimages to the sanctuaries outside the city walls into forms of sacralisation of the rural space and to forms of taking ritual ownership of the term by urban powers, both civil and religious (Vauchez, 2003, 280-281, 298). In this respect, the insistence of cooperation between the city's chapter and senate as representatives of diocesan and council powers highlights the negotiations between both powers that characterises civic religion.

In rarer cases, a cult arises from the action of a specific local or ethnic group and is not a response from the entire urban community. According to Friar Agostinho de Santa Maria this is what happened in Lagos in the Algarve. Here the Sicilian merchant brotherhood established the chapel of Our Lady of Porto Salvo at an unknown date, but certainly before the kingdom of D. Sebastião (1568-1578). The foreign colony was numerous at that time in the Algarve town due to the tuna fishing and trade. The invocation of Mary (who has the same name as the famous sanctuary in Palermo) was protection both for the commercial and sea activity as well as a factor in social distinction for the Italians, as "*they will not allow into their Brotherhood any person from other nations outside the Italian nation*" (Santa Maria, 1716, 463). Even after the tuna fishing industry's deterioration during the sixteenth century and the corresponding reduction of non-Portuguese citizens in Lagos, the brotherhood had by then begun to admit "*some Spaniards*" but no Portuguese citizens, a proof of its identity trait: national exclusivism.

There is such a strong relationship between the devotion to Our Lady of Porto Salvo, the Sicilian brotherhood and tuna fishing that according to Friar Agostinho the decline of all three happens at the same time. By 1599, the chapel would eventually be given to the religious order of the Holy Trinity: "*as the fisheries began to lack, so did the Sicilians (because they were leaving the land) and with them lacked the devotion to the Lady*". The data we have on tuna fishing in the Algarve confirms this picture. According to Joaquim Romero de Magalhães, the Sicilian fishermen and merchants arrived on the Algarve's western coast at the end of the fifteenth century and revolutionised the fishing activity thanks to their long experience in wooden barrel salt curing and preservation. They are the ones responsible for an "enormous increase in fishing profits", despite the very high taxes of 60% or even 70% on the final product, exporting in large quantities to Italy. The beginning of the sixteenth century however, sees a progressive decline in tuna with a corresponding departure of the Sicilian community. Moreover, when a century later the tuna migratory flow returns to the coast of the Algarve, it is the Catalan merchants that will dominate the business (Magalhães, 2012, 258). Neither the tuna fishing nor Our Lady of Porto Salvo returns to Sicilian hands.

Conclusion

The public cult of the saints receives, largely but not exclusively, its canonical form during the medieval time and at the beginning of the modern age from the Christianisation of popular religion. That Christianisation is especially focused on the negotiation of the domination of time, of space, of gestures, and of objects mobilised by the folk culture in order to guarantee supernatural protection against natural threats. From there are born Christian rites carried out around certain times of the year especially the solstices (rogations), in places linked to the manifestation of the sacred (pilgrimages), or of activities especially dependent on nature's favour. One of the Church's most consistent and successful strategies in the Christianisation of popular cults is their own framework and the organisation of intermediate powers such as municipalities and brotherhoods.

Bibliography

Almeida, M.L. & Basto, A.M. (1990) *Crónica de D. João I de Fernão Lopes*. II, Livraria Civilização, Porto.

Amado, T. (1993a) *Crónica de D. João I.* In: Lanciani, G. & Tavani, G. (eds), *Dicionário da Literatura Medieval Galega e Portuguesa.* Caminho, Lisbon, 180-182.

Amado, T. (1993b) *Fernão Lopes.* In: Lanciani, G. & Tavani, G. (ed.), *Dicionário da Literatura Medieval Galega e Portuguesa.* Caminho, Lisbon, 271-273.

Baschet, J. (1999) *Le Diable.* In: Le Goff, J. & Schmitt, J.-C. (ed.), *Dictionnaire Raisonné de l`Occident Médiévale.* Fayard, Paris.

Baschet, J. (2006) *La Civilisation Féodale. De l´An Mil à la Colonisation de l`Amérique.* 3rd ed., Flammarion, Paris.

Beirante, M.A. (1995) *Évora na Idade Média.* Fundação Calouste Gulbenkian/JNICT, Lisbon.

Beirante, M.A. (2007) *O Ar da Cidade. Ensaios de História Medieval e Moderna.* Colibri, Lisbon.

Beirante, M.A. (2011) *Territórios do Sagrado. Crenças e Comportamentos na Idade Média em Portugal.* Colibri, Lisbon.

Benvenuti, A. *et al.* (2005) *Storia della Santitá nel Critianesimo Occidentale.* Viella, Rome.

Bilou, F. (2005) *O Sistema Viário na Antiga Região de Évora.* 2nd ed., Colibri, Lisbon.

Boesch-Gajano, S. (1999) *Sainteté.* In: Le Goff, J. & Schmitt, J-C. (ed.), *Dictionnaire Raisonné de l`Occident Médiévale.* Fayard, Paris.

Boudon, R. (2001) La Rationalité du Religieux Selon Max Weber. *L`Anée Sociologique*, **51**, 9-50.

Briggs, C. (2011) *The Body Broken. Medieval Europe. 1300-1520*, Routledge, London

Brown, P. (1980) *The Cult of the Saints. Its Rise and Function in Latin Christianity.* The University of Chicago Press, Chicago.

Christian, W. (1991) *Religiosidad Local en la España de Felipe II.* Nerea, Madrid

Coelho, M. H. (2011) *A Festa – A Convivialidade.* In: Mattoso, J. (ed.) *História da Vida Privada em Portugal. A Idade Média.* Temas e Debates/Círculo de Leitores, 144-169.

Daveau, S. (1998) *Portugal Geográfico.* 2nd ed., João Sá da Costa.

Duchet-Suchaux, G. & Pastoureau, M. (1994) *La Bible et les Saints. Guide Iconographique.* Flammarion, Paris.

Duffy, E. (2005) *The Stripping of the Altars. Traditional Religion in England c. 1400-c. 1580.* 2nd ed., Yale University Press, New Haven.

Durkheim, E. (1912) *Les Formes Élémentaires de la Vie Religieuse.* Librairie Felix Alcan, Paris.

Espírito Santo, M. (1990) *A Religião Popular Portuguesa.* 2nd ed., Assírio e Alvim, Lisbon.

Farmer, D. (2003) *The Oxford Dictionary of Saints.* 5th ed., Oxford University Press, Oxford.

Fialho, M. & Fonseca, F. (1728), *Évora Gloriosa*. Oficina Komarekiana, Rome.

Garcia y Garcia, A. (1982) *Synodicon Hispanum*. II, Biblioteca de Autores Cristianos, Madrid.

Gouveia, A.C. (2001) *Procissões*. In: Azevedo, C.M. (ed.), *Dicionário de História Religiosa de Portugal*. P-V, Círculo de Leitores, Lisbon, 61-72.

Howard-Johnston, J. & Hayward, P.A. (1999) *The Cult of Saints in Late Antiquity and the Early Middle Ages*. Oxford University Press, Oxford.

Lauwers, M. (1987) Religion Populaire, Culture Folklorique, Mentalités. Notes Pour une Anthropologie Culturelle du Moyen Âge. *Revue d`Histoire Ecclésiastique*, **82,** 228-258.

Kieckeffer, R. (1996) *The Holy and the Unholy. Sainthood, Witchcraft and Magic in Late Medieval Europe*. In: Waugh, S. & Diehl, P. (ed.), *Christendom and Its Discontents. Exclusion, Persecution and Rebellion. 1000-1500.* Cambridge University Press, Cambridge, 310-317.

Krus, L. (2011) *A Construção do Passado Medieval. Textos Inéditos e Publicados*. Instituto de Estudos Medievais, Lisbon.

Le Goff, J. (1977) *Pour Une Autre Moyen Âge. Temps, Travail et Culture En Occident*. Gallimard, Paris.

Le Roy Ladurie, E. (1982) *Montaillou, Village Occitan de 1294 à 1324*. Gallimard, Paris.

Magalhães, J.R. (2012) *O Algarve na Época Moderna*. Imprensa da Universidade de Coimbra, Coimbra.

Markus, R. A. (1998) *The End of Ancient Christianity*. Cambridge University Press, Cambridge.

Marques, A.H.O. (1987) *A Sociedade Medieval Portuguesa*, 5th ed., Livraria Sá da Costa, Lisbon.

Mattoso, J. (2009) *Naquele Tempo. Ensaios de História Medieval.* Temas e Debates/Círculo de Leitores, Lisbon.

Mauss, M. (1902-1903) Esquisse d`Une Théorie Générale de la Magie. *L`Année Sociologique,* **7**, 1-146.

Moita, A.J. (1927) *O Culto de Maria no Patriarcado*. União Gráfica, Lisbon.

Muir, E. (1997) *Ritual in Early Modern Europe*. Cambridge University Press, Cambridge.

Nascimento, A. (1997) *Instrução Pastoral Sobre Superstições Populares. De Correctione Rusticorum*. Cosmos, Lisbon.

Oliveira, E.V. (1995) *Festividades Cíclicas em Portugal*. 2nd ed., Dom Quixote, Lisbon.

Ribeiro, O. (1945) *Portugal, o Mediterrâneo e o Atlântico*. Coimbra Editora, Coimbra.

Rodrigues, A.M. (2000) *A Permanência das Superstições e a Diabolização da Feitiçaria.* In: Azevedo, C.M. (ed.), *História Religiosa de Portugal.* 1, Círculo de Leitores, Lisbon, 43-51.

Ryan, W.G. (1993), *Jacobus de Voragine`s Golden Legend. Readings on the Saints*, I, Princeton University Press, Princeton.

Santa Maria, A. (1716) *Santuário Mariano.* VI, Oficina de António Pedroso Galvam, Lisbon.

Santana, F. & Sucena, E. (1994) *Dicionário de História de Lisboa.* Carlos Quintas e Associados, Lisbon.

Schmitt, J.-C. (1988a) *Religione, Folklore ed Societá nell`Occidente Medievale*. Laterza, Rome.

Schmitt, J.-C. (1988b) *Les Superstitions.* In: Le Goff, J. & Rémond, R. (ed.), *Histoire de la France Religieuse*, I, Seuil, Paris, 417-551.

Schmitt, J.-C. (2001) *Le Corps, les Rites, les Rêves, le Temps. Essai d`Anthropologie Médiévale*. Gallimard, Paris.

Schmitt, J.-C. (2004) *Le Saint Lévrier. Guinefort, Guérisseur d`Enfants Depuis le XIIIe Siècle*. 2nd ed., Flammarion, Paris.

Shinners, J. (2009) *Medieval Popular Religion. 1000-1500. A Reader*. University of Toronto Press, Toronto.

Silva, J.C.V. (2002) A Originalidade e a Homogeneidade do Tardo-Gótico Alentejano. *A Cidade de Évora*, **II-6**, 289-299.

Simplício, M.D. (2002) Évora: Algumas Etapas Fundamentais da Evolução da Cidade Até ao Século XVI. *A Cidade de Évora*, **II-6**, 97-112.

Van Engen, J. (1983) The Christian Middle Ages As an Historiographical Problem. *The American Historical Review*, **91/3**, 519-552.

Vauchez, A. (1988a) *La Sainteté en Occident aux Derniers Siècles du Moyen Age*. École Française de Rome, Rome.

Vauchez, A. (1988b) *Liturgie et Culture Folklorique. Les Rogations Dans la Légende Dorée de Jacques de Voragine*. In: *Fêtes et Liturgie. Actes du Colloque*. Casa de Velásquez, Madrid, 21-34.

Vauchez, A. (2003) *Esperienze Religiose nell Medioevo*. Viella, Rome.

Ventura, M. G. (2003) *Estudos Sobre o Poder. Séculos XIV-XVI.* I, Colibri, Lisbon.

Weber, M. (2001[1904-1905]) *A Ética Protestante e o Espírito do Capitalismo.* 5th ed., Lisboa, Presença, 94 ss.

Wintering in the mountains. How difficulties turned into economic opportunities.

Ana Isabel Queiroz

IELT - Instituto de Estudos de Literatura Tradicional [Institute for Studies of Traditional Literature - Heritages, Arts and Cultures, Faculdade de Ciências Sociais e Humanas], Universidade NOVA de Lisboa

Abstract

This chapter examines how snow and wind have been perceived differently throughout the twentieth century using the mountains of northern Portugal as a case study. The analysis integrates literary readings on exposure to extreme weather (*ca.* 1940) with other sources to observe the transformation of harsh weather conditions into development opportunities for mountain tourism and wind farms.

Keywords: literary landscapes, tourism, wind farms, landscape changes

Introduction

Literary texts and weather qualitative data

Weather and its relation with the territory and inhabitants (flora and fauna, including humans) have always been an elected research topic for geographers and ecologists. In recent years, environmental historians have also reflected on this determinant parameter of natural and cultural histories, finding new results to research on landscape changes and human societies.

One of the leading American environmental historians mentioned weather as a relevant component of the historical relation of humans to nature:
'*Historians seemed to have forgotten completely that, until very recently, almost all people lived as intimately with other species and with the wind as weather as they did with their own kind*' (Worster 1993, preface vii).

Objectives

LITESCAPE.PT – *Atlas of the Literary Landscapes of mainland Portugal* (http://paisagensliterarias.ielt.org/) is a project that aims to link literature and territory, exploring literary works as a source of material for interdisciplinary research. In its framework, this paper deals with weather descriptions in literary texts from the twentieth century and the change in the perception towards strong winds and snowfall since then in two mountain ranges of the Mediterranean biogeographic region[1]: Serra da Estrela (1993 metres high), the highest mountain in mainland Portugal; and the Marão-Alvão range (1,415 metres high).

Among others, Portuguese writers Miguel Torga (1907 – 1995) and Ferreira de Castro (1898 – 1974) portrayed in their stories and novels the living conditions of the rural communities that inhabited the highest mountains of mainland Portugal.

Despite warm wet winters and hot dry summers, weather is dependent on altitude, orientation and distance from the sea. In the mountains, weather is generally unstable: unexpectedly, a storm can roll in and temperatures can drop abruptly. Wind is related to the gradient of pressure and, for that reason, it blows upwards to the mountains and at their summit. Furthermore, temperature on the mountains becomes colder the higher the altitude gets. Air becomes thinner and is less able to absorb and retain heat. The cooler the temperature the less evaporation, meaning that there is more moisture in the air.

In the first half of the twentieth century, these harsh weather conditions, which are a naturally occurring phenomenon, endangered housing, livelihoods and people, particularly during winter. They were also a threat to local agriculture, which is almost the one and only food source, and the most relevant income source.

Using writings from Miguel Torga and Ferreira de Castro as the incipit of a historical narrative about how people perceived harsh weather conditions, this essay explores contemporary attitudes related to wind and snow. These harsh conditions are currently understood as development opportunities for wind power exploitation (all around the northern mountains and coastal areas) and for mountain tourism (in Serra da Estrela).

Taken as a case study, this process of evolution of the perception of weather conditions can be compared and contrasted with observations in other mountainous regions of southern Europe. Here the driving forces of landscape change have had simultaneous and / or similar processes.

Analysis

Suffering winter

In spite of the moderate altitude of Portuguese northern mountains, people from the first half of the twentieth century were harshly exposed to weather extremes during winter. Poor housing, inadequate clothing, insufficient diet or famine, outdoor work and lack of transportation implied an impressive degree of suffering to rural communities.

***Contos da Montanha* (1941) and *Novos Contos da Montanha* (1947), by Miguel Torga**

Contos da Montanha (1941, 1st edition) and *Novos Contos da Montanha* (1947, 1st edition) are two collections of stories by Miguel Torga, focused on remote mountain areas in the Marão-Alvão range (Vila Real district), where he was born and lived his infancy. In these stories, weather is a powerful and frequent element of his literary landscape. Most of these writings portrayed the winter living conditions of villagers, facing difficulties in their daily agro-pastoral activities. In the preface of *Contos da Montanha* (fourth edition, published in 1968) the writer commented on the social and political content of his stories and the four decades of oppression that, he wrote, disfigured the landscape, the human one and the other. He was referring to the period of the "Estado Novo", the dictatorial regime that governed Portugal from 1926 to 1974.

His descriptions are about how people perceived harsh weather conditions. They are presented as an everyday occurrence in rural life during winter. 'Invernia' is the Portuguese term for wintering. It refers to low temperature, rainfall, wind and moisture:
'*A noite estava de invernia. Sobre o telhado caíam bátegas rijas de chuva. E como a casa era de pedra solta e telha vã, cheia de frestas, o vento, que parecia o diabo, de vez em quando entrava por um buraco a assobiar, passava cheio de humidade pela chama da candeia, que se torcia toda, e sumia-se por debaixo da porta como um fantasma*' ("O Cavaquinho" 217)

In this excerpt, he mentioned a harsh storm. The wind seems the devil. It entered through a hole and hissed; it was full of moisture; it disappeared under the door like a ghost. In the same story, the writer also mentions an intense fog: '*o nevoeiro (...) descera agora espesso e molhado sobre o povo*' ("O Cavaquinho" 219). A thick and wet fog came down. The writer played with the double meaning of the Portuguese term 'povo'. The construction '*sobre o povo*' - that can be translated as 'over the village' or as 'over the people' – may suggest a direct injury to the characters. In another story from the same collection, the meteorological elements also strike at people: '*Fria já de si, a Montanha naquele ano encaramelara de vez. Punha-se o nariz de fora da porta, e as espadanadas do ribeiro eram lágrimas de gelo a trespassar-nos. Mas que remédio senão levar o gado à serra, a pastar o sincelo!*' ("Maio Moço" 244).

The narrator, immersed in the frozen landscape, felt the stream drops as piercing tears of ice. Locals take the cattle to the mountains for grazing on the frost. All life in the mountains faced the limits of survival: '*(...) corre por estes montes um vento de miséria que não deixa florir as urzes nem pastar os rebanhos*' (2nd edition preface, *Novos contos da Montanha* 457). A wind of misery blows through these hills, and it does not let the heather bloom nor the livestock graze, Torga wrote.

Nature and culture are fused in a literary landscape which highlights the close relation between all living beings - plants, animals, and humans -, under the same physical conditions. The wind is used as a metaphor for the set of difficulties: the wind transports more than air, it is a vehicle for misery. Weather-related risks to wealth and livelihoods are causes for concern.

The writer used a specific language for qualifying the winter. It is threatening, severe, violent, dark, cold, stormy and wet. Only in spring, when the heather blooms in purple, will the hills loss their brutality: '*Os montes era um gosto vê-los. Cobertos de urze, roxos, tinham perdido a força bruta que o Janeiro lhes dera*' ("A Ladainha" 274).

Despite bad feelings towards the wintering season, Torga added a strong aesthetic dimension to his discourse about the snowy landscape: '*Em Janeiro, então, quem não é cego da alma e, de lá, vê tudo em redor coberto de neve pura, mesmo que seja pastor e tenha o gado na loja morto com fome, acaba por acreditar que a terra foi gerada só para ser possível uma brancura assim*' ("Um filho" 227).

In January, he wrote, those who do not have a blind soul and see the surroundings covered with pure snow believe that the earth was created only so that we were able to witness such pure whiteness. This happens, he continued, although the largest richness of the population was dying of famine: cattle have nothing to eat. In spite of the harshness, the beauty of the white landscape was celebrated.

Torga's literary landscapes can be located in the Continental North climatic province, one of the eleven climatic provinces identified in mainland Portugal by Lautensach (1994). Winters are long and cold, with occasional snow. Climatological data show that from October to March the average minimum temperature is below 0°C (data from Vila Real (1971-2000), *Instituto de Meteorologia website*: http://www.meteo.pt/pt/).

When these stories were published, Vila Real's district had 80.4% of active men working in agriculture (INE 1945). In addition, Torga's characters are mostly peasants and shepherds. He described traditional agro-ecosystems based on a predominantly subsistence strategy in which what people cultivated, they themselves consumed. Nature and its elements were part of their daily life, with a natural exposure to cold and wind. His qualitative records of weather, reproduced by memory, create a physical and psychological uncomfortable scenario. Winter was a time of suffering.

Influenced by Torga's vivid descriptions, his readers may feel the experience of living in the mountains, hungry, poorly clothed, in a house without insulation, walking across a ridge during a storm, having cold and being afraid. These texts send readers on a time travel to the first half of the twentieth century with no bucolic endearment at all.

A Lã e a Neve (1947), by Ferreira de Castro

Ferreira de Castro wrote *A Lã e a Neve* (1947, 1st edition), a novel about people that inhabited Serra da Estrela. It is believed that this mountain range corresponds to what the ancient Romans called Herminius Mons, in homage to Hermes, the Latin-Greek god of the shepherds, also known as Mercury. Two main settlements border the literary landscape of *A Lã e a Neve*: Covilhã (altitude=450-800 metres) and Manteigas (altitude = 775 metres). In addition, a dual meaning in the title refers to two driving elements of the novel: the wool ('*a lã*') and the snow ('*a neve*').

Covilhã is located on the southeast slope of Serra da Estrela. Because of its relevance in wool manufacturing, it was the more prominent town in the region. Manteigas was a smaller town in the heart of the mountain, located in the glacial valley of the Zêzere River (here still a very small stream near to its source). It also had a small secondary industry related to sheep herding with dairy products, as butter ('manteiga', like the village name) and cheese.

In 1940, Covilhã was the most populous municipality in the Castelo Branco District, with 60 434 inhabitants. It distinguished itself from the other 10 counties by people density (110 inhabitants per km^2) and because only 35.6% of active men worked in agriculture (in the others, the percentage was around 70%) (INE, 1944). These data reflect the importance of the industry, which is a subject matter in Ferreira de Castro's novel.

In the novel, *Horácio* and *Serafim* take walk from Manteigas to Covilhã. It is a long crossing through hills and valleys: four hours without snow, five or more with it, the writer wrote. They left the small town after 7 p.m., passed the river and entered into an isolated and sloping area. Night falls, and they are caught in a snowstorm: *'A neve aumentava, rodopiava em volta deles, fustigando-os sem cessar (203-4) (...) naquele mar de leite cristalizado (208) (...) a neve deformara tudo, covas e relevos, pedras e urzes, igualando, em longos trechos, o que, noutros dias e noutras noites, era diferente (209)'.*

The snow increased, whirled around them, harassing them continually. It resembles a sea of crystallized milk, evening out the landscape that in other days and nights was quite different. Without land references, the characters get lost. In those harsh weather conditions, the mountain is frightening. The strong icy wind is the cause of their fear, exhaustion and despair:

'[U]m vento gelado (...) a entoar um lamento cada vez mais forte e prolongado. Depois, largara-se a uivar, não se sabia em que profundas cavernas, que lhe avolumavam o desespero errante (203) (...) O vento... continuava a dominar tudo com os seus uivos, que mantinham a alma da noite num perpétuo estarrecimento (212)'.

He mentions a frosty wind that sings a lament increasingly strong and prolonged, and dominates everything with its howls. Like a wolf, the terror inspiring mountain animal, this wind howls.

Serra da Estrela is located in the Northern Mountains climatic province (Lautensach 1994). Winter is cold and snowy. Unpredictable storms are frequent and severe. The writer reproduced the natural elements and the feelings of experiencing them.

Later on in the story, *Júlia*, *Ricardo* and their children are at home in Aldeia do Carvalho, a village near Covilhã. They are in bed, but they cannot sleep because of low temperatures. "I'm cold" is a repeated sentence in the text:

- Mãe! Ó mãe! Eu tenho frio!

Lá em baixo, os outros filhos de Ricardo despertaram e alguns deles gritaram com o irmão:

- Eu também tenho! Eu também tenho frio.

Júlia acendeu a luz e berrou-lhes que se calassem. Em seguida, ergueu-se e colocou sobre os filhos quanto trapo havia em casa. Mas ela via bem que aquilo não chegava. Ela própria tremia de frio. (236)

Much like the stories of Miguel Torga, exposure to the hardship of wintering resulted from poor living conditions. Except for a few privileged, the entire population of Serra da Estrela (whether shepherds or workers in the wool mills) was in the same scenario of discomfort and misery. The prosperity of the wool industry was supported by the stunted cost of production, due to low salaries and no social protection, and was labouring with outdated technology. These aspects are also described in the novel.

Changes in mountain counties

A few decades after the literary descriptions of Torga and Ferreira de Castro, major changes could be recorded in demography, agriculture and industry in the mountain counties. In the town of Sabrosa (the county where Torga was born), electric power arrived only in 1932 and several decades went by until all the villages of the county had the same commodity (Soares, 2005). From 1940 to 2010, Sabrosa lost 52% of its inhabitants (n=6421) (INE 1945; INE website). This municipality faced a continuous decline throughout the last century, with a clear break between 1960 and 1991 (12903 inhabitants reduced to 7478), due to emigration to foreign countries, particularly to France (Soares, 2005). Between 1989 and 1999, the number of farmers was still decreasing, following the same tendency throughout the whole Portuguese territory; the resident population was also aging (most farmers were over 55 years old) (Pinto-Correia *et al.*, 2006).

From 1940 to 2010, Covilhã lost 16% of its inhabitants (n=51 145) (INE 1944; *INE website*). In 1962, there were still 133 wool production factories (compared to 172 in 1940), virtually all using mechanical technology (Pinto, 1963). In 1985, national authorities commissioned a study on restructuring the sector: the largest employers are not viable because of excess of workers and obsolete technology (Ministério da Indústria e Comércio 1987). Restructuring never occurred and the project was overtaken by global economic dynamics. The wool industry went into decline, until it attained the vestigial relevance it has today.

In the rural territory of Portugal, particularly from the 1960s onwards, people left part of their isolation and obscurity, a process driven by improved communications and transportation, increasing movement of people and national television coverage (Barreto, 1996). Savings from immigrants contributed to the improvement of food and housing of the population that had hitherto survived the vicissitudes of nature, practicing subsistence farming and domestic consumption. This enhancement is still significant in the following decades, because of the change of political regime in 1974, the implementation of social policies on health and education, and Portugal's adherence to the EEC in 1986.

All throughout this period of social transformation, a profound change in the relationship between people and nature occurred. Exposure to weather elements decreases with the improvement of the living conditions of mountain populations. Low temperatures combined with strong winds, which increases the perception of cold, were tolerated. Better food, better clothing, thermal comfort indoors, and less outdoor activities in bad weather, contributed to a change in the way people perceive them.

Beloved wind: the wind energy production in Portugal

In the last decades of the twentieth century, when and where the wind is blowing hard, its negative relevance in daily life was either accepted or ignored. Today, on the contrary, the wind is positively recognised for its energy and appreciated by the economic value it generates, both at national and local level.

Windmills for mechanical power and sails to propel ships are ancient forms of the wind's potential uses. In the 1980s, the first wind turbines were installed to produce electricity. It is a renewable form of energy with no greenhouse gas emissions during production. Portugal was one of Europe's pioneers in the field: two wind farms were built on island territories: Porto Santo (Madeira, 1986) and Santa Maria (Azores, 1988). However, the high potential wind power also identified in the mainland, particularly in some coastal areas and in the central and northern mountains soon motivated a fast growing activity of independent energy producers, especially in the less populated interior.

In the last three decades, the Portuguese national authorities also valued wind as a resource. Renewable energy, including that of the wind, is from then a central issue in environmental and economic policy and a major contributor to independent energy production. Wind power (the green bars in Figure 1) has been growing fast since 2001. In February 2010, Portugal was ranked the sixth European producer and the ninth World producer of wind power (Castro 2011).

In 2008, Portugal defined an ambitious target for wind power production: 5100 MW installed up to the end of 2012. Beyond the European Union climate-energy legislative policy (Directive 2009/28/EC adopted on the April 6), the Portuguese legal package includes a streamlining of administrative procedures and the introduction of tariffs for the sale of energy, based on a very attractive remuneration[3].

It drove a continuous increase of the number of wind farms, turbines and installed power, slowed down only by the economical crisis of the last two years. A similar growth process occurred in Spain and Italy, among other countries.

Figure 1. Energy delivered by Portuguese independent producers between 2000 and 2011, per technology [GWh]; green bars correspond to wind power (from ERSE *website*).

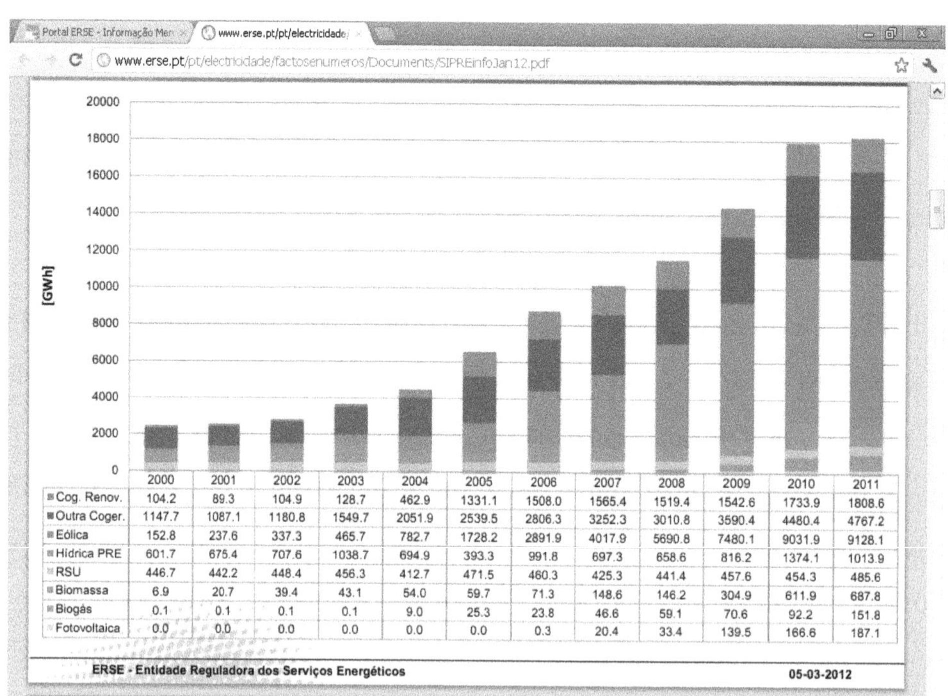

	2000	2001	2002	2003	2004	2005	2006	2007	2008	2009	2010	2011
Cog. Renov.	104.2	89.3	104.9	128.7	462.9	1331.1	1508.0	1565.4	1519.4	1542.6	1733.9	1808.6
Outra Coger.	1147.7	1087.1	1180.8	1549.7	2051.9	2539.5	2806.3	3252.3	3010.8	3590.4	4480.4	4767.2
Eólica	152.8	237.6	337.3	465.7	782.7	1728.2	2891.9	4017.9	5690.8	7480.1	9031.9	9128.1
Hídrica PRE	601.7	675.4	707.6	1038.7	694.9	393.3	991.8	697.3	658.6	816.2	1374.1	1013.9
RSU	446.7	442.2	448.4	456.3	412.7	471.5	460.3	425.3	441.4	457.6	454.3	485.6
Biomassa	6.9	20.7	39.4	43.1	54.0	59.7	71.3	148.6	146.2	304.9	611.9	687.8
Biogás	0.1	0.1	0.1	0.1	9.0	25.3	23.8	46.6	59.1	70.6	92.2	151.8
Fotovoltaica	0.0	0.0	0.0	0.0	0.0	0.0	0.3	20.4	33.4	139.5	166.6	187.1

The policy for energy is shrouded in criticism, supported by economical and environmental arguments: financial incentives to the producers increase the final price of energy to consumers, and, being located on mainly natural areas, wind farms have impacts on landscape and biodiversity. The areas described in literary writings belong to the EU Natura 2000 network (ICNB *webpage*, Rede Natura 2000) due to the presence of significant biodiversity values, such as natural habitats, flora and fauna protected species (respectively from the appendix I and II of Habitats Directive). Its conservation status, that is potentially a constraint to licensing wind farms, has not prevented wind farms' approval after environmental impact assessments.

On a local scale, wind farms are generally welcome. For installing them, energy producers usually lease land in order to obtain an annual income. In the Northern mountains, these are almost all commons ('baldios' in Portuguese, lands managed by local people who hold their rights in common), which had lost their ancient economical relevance for local people through the process of land abandonment described above. This rent is low cost to producers but a significant source of income for management authorities (e.g. civil parish councils) who receive and administer it. In this context, it is not surprising the general favourable attitude of local people, who perceive wind as an economic opportunity.

Beloved snow: Herminius Mons tourism

Since the last decades of the nineteenth century, Serra da Estrela has aroused the interest of scientists and pioneers in the discovery of remote territories. It was already visited in the temperate season and promoted by its aesthetic panoramas and healing properties (Abreu, 1905). Travel books and official propaganda renamed the ancient Herminius Mons, the pastoral territory still crossed by sheep flocks, as "National Switzerland". It recalled the air purity, the water quality, the beauty of snowy mountain landscapes. Winter tourism developed, however, after the establishment of the Initiative Committee of Covilhã - Comissão de Iniciativa da Covilhã in 1929. Looking at the climatic characteristics of the mountain, unique in the national context, this Committee promoted a better quality of hostels and hotels and the opening of new accesses throughout the mountain, imperative conditions for recreational activities and winter sports (its labour was exhaustively studied by Silva 2005).

Snow sports were then widespread in Europe: the first Winter Olympic Games occurred in Chamonix (France) in 1924 and the first Alpine World Championship was held in 1931. In 1933, the Ski Club of Portugal ("Esqui Clube de Portugal") opened its first office in Serra da Estrela and organised the first official races in 1935, followed by the first National Championship in 1938 (Pimentel, 2005).

Winter visitors were a notorious presence in Covilhã in the early years of World War II. This new phenomenon is described in *A Lã e a Neve*:
Nos planaltos da serra a neve subira já muitos palmos e, então, como todos os anos, começaram a passar pela Covilhã rapazes e raparigas, filhos de gente endinheirada, que vinham de Lisboa fazer esqui. Traziam, por mor do tempo, muitos abafos, grossas blusas, que se fabricavam ali. (...) os rapazes e as raparigas partiam para o alto da serra, para o Hotel das Penhas da Saúde. E lá, durante as manhãs e as tardes, eles corriam, com os seus esquis, sobre as longas superfícies nevadas, sobre os longos declives brancos, volteia aqui, tomba ali, ergue acolá, e os seus alegres risos iam quebrando o gelado silêncio da montanha. (346).

For those who did not face cold unprotected or on a daily basis - sons and daughters of wealthy people, who came from Lisbon, Ferreira de Castro wrote -, snow generated curiosity and it was a medium of pleasure and fun. The landscape had ceased to frighten the spirits, wrote the representative of the Initiative Committee of Covilhã in the minutes of the First National Congress of Tourism (‘*apavorar os espíritos*’, in the original Moura 1936).

In 1956, the Tourism Commission of Covilhã published a brochure with a detailed map of Serra da Estrela where the areas for skiing were identified. One text stated that the winter on the mountain featured special virtues that young and old could enjoy. Long walks on the snowy slopes were recommended as an excellent exercise to build muscles, extend chest and reinforce nerves (CMTC, 1956).

In the 1970s, against what until then seemed a unanimous opinion, some voices claimed the tourist development of Serra da Estrela could never be based on winter sports (Simões, 1976). Its defenders supports that the reduced number of days with snow on the ground and good visibility for skiing compromise the sustainability of an investment. On the contrary, he suggested that the maintenance and recovering of the equipment already installed while other local leisure interests were being promoted.

The snow was then perceived as a precious, but scarce resource. After it had proved too much for the extremely exposed local populations and motivated the interest for winter tourism, snow seemed to be, in those days, an insufficient element to support tourism in the area.

A growing concern regarding the environmental impacts of mass-market tourism on landscape and wildlife led to the classification of Serra da Estrela Natural Park in 1976. Such a park was aimed at preserving the cultural characteristics of the mountain populations and unique landscapes, ice-shaped at the time of glaciers, high mountain habitats and endemic flora, and fauna species adapted to the harsh winter weather, the major nature conservation values in the area[4].

Tourism in Serra da Estrela remained, to the present, associated with public and private entities with a close connection to the regional economy. Since 1971, the *Turistrela* Company has the exclusive concession for tourism in the Serra da Estrela. The concession area is approximately one hundred thousand hectares, above the elevation of 800 metres. The monopoly of exploitation was renewed in 1986 for sixty years.

Snow has always been a major attraction, especially to national visitors that have no other place in Portugal to enjoy it. However, the limited conditions for skiing (or even sliding) recommended the installation of a snow-gun, a device for manufacturing snow from pressurized air and water in a ski resort for when there is no production of natural snowfalls.

Nowadays, Covilhã, Manteigas, and other small towns and villages in the area receive thousands of visitors a year. They come to Serra da Estrela all year long, motivated by natural and cultural values, although the snowy landscapes are largely preferred from the Christmas holidays to Easter. It is still an iconic "White Mountain" for Portuguese people and a popular destination for families, in a country where it is often necessary to go on top of this mountain to have a first time view of a snowy mountain landscape.

Final remarks

The image of rural Portugal in the first half of the twentieth century, portrayed by the writings of Miguel Torga and Ferreira de Castro, is inseparable from striking weather elements: low temperatures, rainfall (in the form of rain, snow and ice), and strong winds. For today's readers, especially for those who are not living in the countryside or who are not exposed to the experiences described, literary descriptions of weather adversity may erroneously suggest a climate change. This is not addressed here. In this chapter, wind and snow are not highlighted by their figures or temporal changes (they are intentionally absent). It focuses on the way new responses to them resulted in developments with economic benefits, because of external economic factors that change the social and economic paradigms. Wind and snow made this history or, at least, without them, the story would have been rather different.

References

Abreu, A. (1905) *Serra da Estrela (Guia do Tourista)*. Livraria Ferreira & Oliveira. L.^{da}, Lisbon.

Armiero, M. & Barca, S. (2004) *Storia dell' Ambiente. Una introduzione*. Carocci, Rome.

Avilés, J. (1996) La novela como fuente para la historia: el caso de Crimen y castigo (1866). *Espaço, Tempo y Forma. Historia Contemporánea,* **9**, 337-360.

Barreto, A. (1996) Três décadas de mudança social. Barreto, A. (org.) *A situação social em Portugal, 1960-1995*. Instituto de Ciências Sociais – Universidade de Lisboa, Lisbon.

Cassuto, D. N. (1997) *Turning wine into water: water as privileged signifier*. In *The Grapes of Wrath*. Beegel, S.F., Shillinglaw, S. and Tiffney, Jr., *Steinbeck and the Environment*. The University of Alabama Press, Tuscaloosa.

Castro, R. (2011) *Uma introdução às energias renováveis: eólica, fotovoltaica e mini-hídrica*. Instituto Superior Técnico Press, Lisbon.

Costa, P. (2004) *Atlas do Potencial Eólico para Portugal Continental*. Master Dissertation, Faculdade de Ciências da Universidade de Lisboa, Lisbon. http://194.117.7.100/docs/PauloCostaMSc.pdf

Comissão Municipal de Turismo da Covilhã (1956) *Zonas de ski: circuito da Serra da Estrela*. Comissão Municipal de Turismo da Covilhã, Covilhã.

Donald W. (1993) *Wealth of Nature. Environmental History and the Ecological Imagination*. Oxford University Press, New York and Oxford.

ERSE – Entidade Reguladora dos Serviços Energéticos website. *Factos e Números*. http://www.erse.pt/pt/electricidade/factosenumeros/Paginas/DivulgacaoMensaldeInformacaosobreaPRE.aspx, accessed March 2012.

Ferreira de, C. (1990, 15ª ed.) *A Lã e a Neve*. Guimarães Editores, Lisbon.

Foster, D.R. (2002) Thoreau's country: a historical-ecological perspective on conservation in the New England landscape. *Journal of Biogeography*, **29**, 1537- 1555.

Fuster García, F. (2011) La novela como fuente para la Historia Contemporánea: El árbol de la ciencia de Pío Baroja y la crisis de fin de siglo en España. *Espaço, Tempo y Forma. História Contemporanea,* **23**, 55-72.

Gergis J., Garden, D. & Fenby, C. (2010) The Influence of Climate on the First European Settlement of Australia: A Comparison of Weather Journals, Documentary Data and Palaeoclimate Records, 1788–1793. *Environmental History,* **15**, 485–507.

ICNB – Instituto da Conservação da Natureza e Biodiversidade website. *Rede Natura 2000*. http://portal.icnb.pt/ICNPortal/vPT2007/O+ICNB/Rede+Natura+2000/sitios_importancia_comunitaria.htm, accessed March 2012.

IGEO – Instituto Geográfico Português website. *Atlas de Portugal*. www.igeo.pt/atlas/Images/Cap1/Cap1c_p42.jpg, accessed in March 2012.

INE – Instituto Nacional de Estatística (1944) *VIII Recenseamento Geral da População no continente e ilhas adjacentes em 12 de Dezembro de 1940. Volume XVI – Distrito de Castelo Branco*. Sociedade Astória, Lisbon.

INE – Instituto Nacional de Estatística (1945) *VIII Recenseamento Geral da População no continente e ilhas adjacentes em 12 de Dezembro de 1940. Volume XVIII – Distrito de Vila Real*. Sociedade Tipográfica, Lisbon.

INE – Instituto Nacional de Estatística website. www.ine.pt, accessed in March 2012.

IM - Instituto de Meteorologia website. http://www.meteo.pt/pt/, accessed in March 2012.

Lautensach, H. (1994) As características climáticas. In: Ribeiro, O. & Lautensach, H..*Geografia de Portugal. II O Ritmo climático e a Paisagem (comentários e actualizações de Suzanne Daveau)*, 337-369. Edições João Sá da Costa, Lisbon.

LaCapra, D. (1992) *History and Criticism*. Cornell University Press, New York.

Ministério da Indústria e Comércio (1987) *Estudo da Indústria de Lanifícios da Beira Interior, 3 volumes*. Direcção Geral da Indústria, Lisbon.

Moura, A.M. (1936) *Turismo e Desportos de Inverno*. Soc. Nac. Tipografia : Lisbon.

Pimentel, P. *História do Esqui e o Esqui em Portugal*. www.pimentelonline.com, accessed in March 2012.

Pinto, A. (1963) A Indústria de Lanifícios no ano de 1962. Separata da revista, *Lanifícios*, **163-165**.

Pinto Correia, T.; Breman. B.; Jorge, V. & Dneboská, M. (2006) *Estudo sobre o Abandono em Portugal Continental. Análise das dinâmicas da Ocupação do Solo, do Sector Agrícola e da Comunidade Rural Tipologia de Áreas Rurais*. Universidade de Évora. http://library.wur.nl/WebQuery/clc/1943642

Queiroz, A.I. & Andresen, M.T. (2007) Wild birds in Aquilino Ribeiro's Writings: Using literature as a source for environmental history. In: Aftandilian, D. (ed.) *What are the animals to us?* Tennessee University Press, Knowville.

Queiroz, A.I. (2005) Building landscape memory through combined sources: commons afforestation in Portugal. In: Tress, B., Tress, G., Fry, G. & Opdam, P. (eds). *From Landscape Research to Landscape Planning: Aspects of Integration, Education, and Application*, 335-344. Springer, Dordrecht.

Robertson, M., Nichols, P., Horwitz, P., Bradly, K. & Mackintosh, D. (2000) Environmental narratives and the need for multiple perspectives to restore degraded landscape in Australia. *Ecosystem Health*, **6**, 119–133.

Silbernagel, J., Martin, S., Gale, M. & Chen, J., (1997) Prehistoric, historic, and present settlement patterns related to ecological hierarchy in the Eastern Upper Peninsula of Michigan, USA. *Landscape Ecology* **12**, 223-240.

Silva, S. (2005) *O Turismo na Serra da Estrela: a Comissão de Iniciativa de Covilhã, 1929-1936*. Master dissertation. Universidade de Aveiro. [non-published].

Simões, D. (1976) *Serra da Estrela: bases para programação do seu desenvolvimento turístico*. Author edition, Covilhã.

Soares, A. (2005) *Sabrosa da pré-história à actualidade*. Câmara Municipal de Sabrosa, Sabrosa.

Thomas, K. (1983) *Man and the Natural World*. Penguin, London.

Torga, M. (ed. 2001) *Contos*. Publicações Dom Quixote, Lisbon.

End notes

[1]Biogeographic regions have similar environmental conditions and are capable of harbouring the same type of biota. See on a map the European biogeographic regions: http://www.eea.europa.eu/data-and-maps/data/biogeographical-regions-europe.

[2] Page references are from the altogether stories 1st edition, published in 2010.

[3] Portuguese legal package includes, among others, these three relevant diplomas: Resolução do Conselho de Ministros [Ministry Council Resolution] nº1/2008, de 4 de Janeiro; Decreto-Lei [Law-Decree] nº 225/2007 de 31 de Maio and Decreto-Lei [Law-Decree] nº51/2010 de 20 de Maio.

[4] Serra da Estrela Natural Park was created by the Decreto-Lei [Law-Decree] nº 557/76 de 16 de Julho.

A Fear of Nature: Images & Perceptions of Heath, Moor, Bog & Fen in England

Ian D. Rotherham

Sheffield Hallam University

Macbeth - Scene 1. - A desert Heath

'*When shall we three meet again*
In thunder lightning, or in rain?
When the hurlyburly's done,
When the battle's lost and won,
That will be ere the set of sun,
Where the place?
Upon the heath ……………… Fair is foul and foul is fair,
Hover through the fog and filthy air'

William Shakespeare 1600s

Figure 1. The three witches.

Abstract

The meeting of the three hags or witches upon the desert heath with its fog and foul air both reflects an image of this landscape and impacts indelibly on the psyche of the reader from Shakespeare's time to our own.

Writers from Thomas Pennant and Samuel Johnson in the 1700s, to Alfred Wainwright and H.V. Morton in the 1900s, created and sold images of English landscapes, of people, and culture. Their market was a curious public and especially the growing legions of visitors and tourists. Perceptions and images became central to the writing of novelists such as Thomas Hardy and Daphne Du Maurier. The books that resulted helped create images of cultural landscapes and today they and their works have in turn become a part of visitor attractions and experiences. They are themselves absorbed within and subsumed by that which they in part created. Ouseby (1990) and other researchers have addressed the broad context of these issues, and for specific regions such as Cornwall, papers by Birks (1997), Hughes (1997) and Moody (1997) give a useful insight into how nature, culture and tourism merge.

Figure 2. The desert heath in the storm

For centuries, fens, bogs and heaths were places to avoid unless you were a local who lived in and depended upon the resources of these god-forsaken places. Giblett (1996) describes the perceptions of wetlands:

'*Wetlands are not always, and for some not ever, the most pleasant of places. In fact they have often been seen as horrific places. In the patriarchal western cultural tradition wetlands have been associated with death and disease, the monstrous and the melancholic, if not, the downright mad. Wetlands are 'black waters'. They have even been seen as a threat to health and sanity, to the clean and proper body, and mind. The typical response to the horrors and threats posed by wetlands has been simple and decisive: dredge, drain or fill and so 'reclaim' them. Yet the idea of reclaiming wetlands begs the questions of reclaimed from what? For what? For whom? A critical history of wetlands' drainage could quite easily be entitled 'Discipline and Drain'.*'

Yet today, fear and loathing and myths or histories of wild, dangerous and frightening landscapes, have become the stuff of tourism. Fuelled by literature with the written book, and now by the film versions too, these landscapes and their stories are major tourism destinations and attractants. Understanding the reactions and responses to potentially frightening and dangerous locations and landscapes is important to developing and promoting tourism destinations. I argue that visitors may be drawn to a location equally by myth as by reality.

Keywords: fear, loathing, landscape, wetland, moor, bog, fen, weather, climate

Introduction: fear and loathing

Fear and the environment, or fear of the environment, are often deeply ingrained into the human psyche. Yet we must ask the questions of is this to do with reality or perception, of history or myth? The environment and climate for example can be seen as fearful powers and forces of nature, from storm, flood, tides, tempest, disease and death, wild nature and dangerous fearful terrain, places difficult and dangerous to travel, locations unknown and dark, and populated by strange, wild and dangerous '*foreign*' people. Moreover, there is much both myth and popular culture through the centuries, which adds to this fear and loathing.

Yet the threats were real as well as perceptions. In pre-industrial societies, famine was always close by and could follow on the heels of disaster or bad weather. The eleventh-century *Anglo-Saxon Chronicle* states that following great storms: '.. *Such a malady fell on men that almost every other man was in the worst evil, that is with fever .... And many men died of the evil……through the great tempests which came ...a very great famine all over England, so that many hundred men died through famine.*' Twelfth-century writer Robert de Monte observed '…..*the sea passed over its usual limits, in consequence of which the lands on the coast which has been sown with corn were destroyed in many places.*' Matthew Paris, thirteenth-century writer and commentator described how land was affected by '…. *a great deluge of rain so that the channels of the air were uncovered to the cataracts and the clouds were seen to pour out upon the earth to destroy it*'.

Figure 3. Some of the remaining or past areas of fen, bog, moor and heath

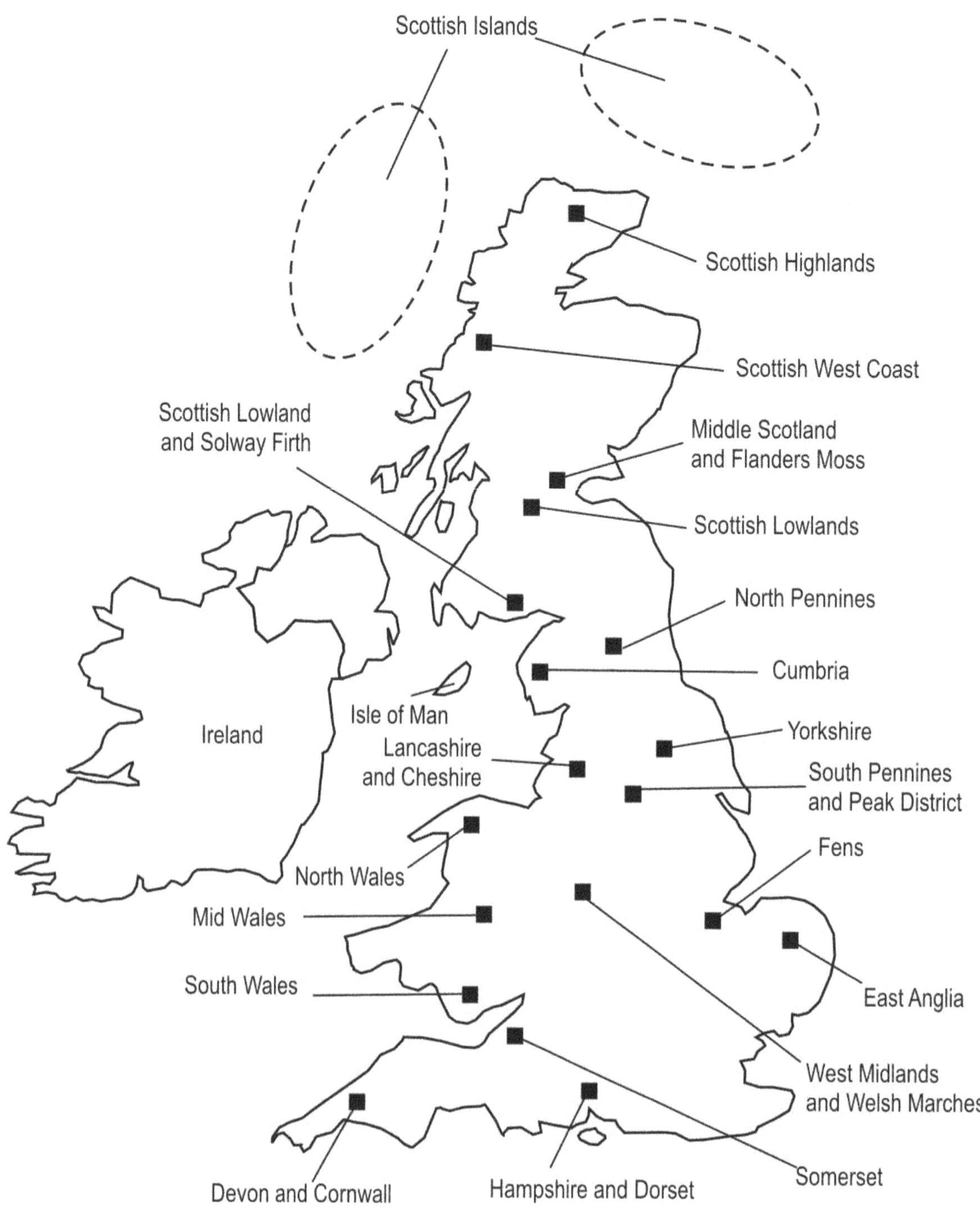

In the once great fenland and peat bog of the Humberhead Levels in South Yorkshire and north Lincolnshire, it is clear that this was a vast and remote area dominated by wetland and water for much of the year. It was both a productive landscape but also an inconvenient and even dangerous one too. As recorded by De La Pryme in late 1687, it was vulnerable to sudden inundations:

'Towards the end of this year (1687) there happened a great inundation on the levels, by means of much rains that fell, and the high tides; which increased the waters so, that they

broke the banks and drowned the country for a vast many miles about. My father, and every one in general that dwelt there, lost very considerably in their winter corn, besides the great expense they were put to by boating their cattle to the hills, and firm lands, with the trouble of keeping them the two or three months. I have been several times upon these banks, (which are about three yards in height,) when the water has been full to the very tops, and nothing appeared on that side but a terrible tempestuous sea. The water remains about half a week, and sometimes a week, at its full height, whose motions some hundreds of people are watching night and day. But if it chance to be so strong, as to drive away, as it often does, any quantity of any of the banks, then it drowns all before it, and makes a noise by its fall which is heard many miles before they perceive the water; and in the places where it precipitates itself down, makes a huge pond or pit, sometimes one hundred yards about, and a vast depth, so that in that place, it being impossible for the bank to be built again, they always build it half round, many of which pits and banks may be seen beyond Thorne.'

Then again, but even worse, on 17th December 1697:

'*.....we had a very great snow, which was on the level ground about two foot and a half thick. After a pretty hard frost, which froze over again for several days. On 20th it thawed exceedingly fast, upon which there came down a great flood that the like was never known; about forty one years since there was the greatest flood that was ever remembered, but that was much less than this; for this came roaring all of a sudden, about eleven o'clock at night, on Bramwith, Fishlake, Thorne, and other towns, upon which all the people rung all their bells backwards (as they commonly do in case of a great fire,) but though this frightened all to the banks, and bid them all look about them, yet, nevertheless, the loss was very great. The people of Sykehouse, and Fishlake, they had banks to save them, yet it overtopt all; drowned the beasts in their folds and destroyed their sheep; several men lost their lives; the houses in Sykehouse and Fishlake being drowned up to the very eaves; so that they reckon no less then £3,000 damage was done by the same in the parish of Fishlake. It came with such force against all the banks about Thorne, which kept the waters off the Levels, that everybody gave them over, there being no hopes to save them, and ran over them all along, a nd the ground being so hard they could not strike down stakes upon the tops of their banks, to hinder the water from running over. At last, it being impossible that such vast waters should be contained in such short small bounds, it burst a huge gime close by Gore Style. Near Thorne, where there had been a vast gime formerly,* *and so drowned the whole levels to an exceeding great depth, so that many people were kept so long in the upper part of their houses that they were almost pined, whilst all their beasts were drowned about them. It was indeed a very sad thing to hear the oxen bellowing and the sheep bleating, and the people crying out for help round about as they did, all over Bramwith, Sykehouse, Stainford, and Fishlake, and undoubtedly in other places, yet no one could get to save or help them, it being about midnight; and so many poor people were forced to remain, for several days together, some upon the tops of their houses, others in the highest rooms, without meat or fire, until they were almost starved.*'

Figure 4. A flood in the Fens

This was not the end of the floods, with at least two or three equally destructive inundations described for the area over the century after De La Pryme. In 1747, G. Stovin esq., wrote a description of Hatfield Chase from a visit accompanied by the Rev. Samuel Wesley: '........*the water of the morass is of the colour of coffee. There is plenty of furze bushes, etc. and variety of game, such as hares, foxes, kites, eagles, curlews, ducks, and geese; ....*' The peat bogs were probably dominated by at least two great 'raised mires' and even after extensive drainage, it was suggested that in 1829 '.....*the depth of the morass near Thorne, in some places is 20 feet thick*'. In the heart of the bog, it could well have been much more.

The vast wilderness areas generated fear and genuine threat too. Moreover, they provided wealth and sustenance in the shadow of the threats. Control and influence or ownership over these areas was also a matter of contention.

Contested landscapes

As David Lowenthal stated so eloquently in 1985, '*The past is a foreign country*'; essentially, today we are foreigners looking in from the outside. However, it is important to realise too, that contemporary writers were also in a similar position. These landscapes were often disputed spaces, and we need to consider them looking in and looking out. This is difficult since the local cultures were often oral not written and the landscapes themselves, and much of their indigenous culture, have largely been erased. Chris Smout (2000) noted '*There are many thousands of hectares of what is now prime arable land, especially in northern England, that were in the 17th century, fen and mire*' and '*.....it is surprising how... Yorkshire fenlands have evaporated from general memory*'.

William Dugdale (1662), as an outsider looking in to drain and '*improve*' the Fens, described the Fen country as '*...For the space of many years until of late years, a vast and deep Fen affording little benefit to the realm other than Fish and Fowl, with over much harbour to a rude and beggarly people.*' Dugdale asked '*...And what expectation of health can there be to the bodies of men, where there is no element good? The air being for the most part cloudy, gross, and full of rotten harrs; the water putrid and muddy, yea, full of loathsome vermin; the earth spungy and boggy, and the fire noisome by the stink of smoaky hassocks*'.

Dugdale in the 1700s quotes an earlier writer on the visit of St Guthlac to Crowland: '*In the middle part of Britain there is a hideous fen of huge bigness, which extends in a very long track even to the sea, oftimes clouded with moist and dark vapours, having within it divers islands and woods, as crooked and winding rivers. When, therefore, that a man of blessed memory, Guthlac, had found out the desert places of this vast wilderness, he inquired of the borderers what they knew thereof. One amongst them, called Tatwaine, stood up amongst them, who affirmed that he knew a certain island in the more remote and secret parts thereof, which many had attempted to inhabit, but could not for the strange and uncouth monsters and several terrors wherewith they were affrighted, wherewith*

Guthlac earnestly entreated that he would show him that place. Tatwaine, therefore, yielding to the request of that holy man, taking a fishing-boat, led thereunto; it being called Crowland, and in respect to its desertness known to very few, by reason that apparitions of devils were so frequently seen there.'

During the night, Guthlac became aware of his cell being: '......*full of black troops of unclean spirits, which crept under the door, as also at chinks and holes, and coming both out of the sky and from the earth, filling the air, as it were, with dark clouds. In their looks they were cruel, and of form terrible – having great heads, ill-favoured beards, rough ears, wrinkled foreheads, fierce eyes, teeth like horses, swollen ankles, preposterous feet, and hoarse cries....*'

Worse was to come: '.....*who with such mighty shrieks were heard to roar, and by-and-by, rushing into the house, first bound the holy man, then drew him out of his cell, and cast him over head and ears into the dirty fen; and, having so done, carried him through the most rough and troublesome parts thereof, drawing him among brambles and briars for the tearing of his limbs.*'

Perhaps Guthlac had succumbed to an attack of the ague and was hallucinating. On the other hand, maybe he was being mugged by the locals or both.

A monastic scribe called Felix writing in the early eighth century of the life of St Guthlac, explained that in the Fens '*There are immense marshes, now a black pool of water, now foul running streams, and also many islands, and reeds, and hillocks, and thickets, and with manifold windings wide and long it continues to the north sea.*'

We have eye-witness accounts of the impact of a tsunami on Somerset on January 20th 1606 '..... *An inundation of the sea water by overflowing and breaking down the sea banks ......many persons were drowned and much cattle and goods were lost.*' And there were '....*huge and mighty hills of water ...as if the greatest mountains in the world had overwhelmed the lowest valleys.... faster than the birds could fly......*'. Hundreds of people drowned and thousands of sheep and cattle perished.

In early modern Europe, marshes and fens were perceived as places of fear and loathing. Shrouded in King Lear's '*fen-sucked fogs*', they were unsafe and evil wastes where drowning was common. One could be poisoned by the corrupted waters or by the foul air, contracting the '*ague*' or marsh malaria. Until the late nineteenth century, this widespread disease was thought to originate in the bad air (mal-aria) of these stagnant wetlands. In 1629, one tract urging the draining of the East Anglian Fens described them as sunk in '*water putred and muddy, yea full of loathsome vermin; the earth, spuing, unfast and boggie*'.

Dr Adam Mercer (1505) described the fens as: '... *one of the most brute and beastly of the whole realm, a land of marshy ague and unwholesome swamps.*' Macaulay in his *History of England* suggested that the area between Cambridge and the Wash was '...*a vast and desolate fen, saturated with all the moisture of thirteen centuries, and overhung during the greater part of the year by a low grey mist, above which rose, visible many miles, the magnificent tower of Ely. In that dreary region, covered by vast flights of wild-fowl, a half-savage population, known by the name of breedlings, there led an amphibious life, sometimes wading, sometimes rowing, from one islet of firm ground to the other. The roads were amongst the worst in the island.*'

Yet today, contemporary landscapes of heaths, commons, moors, bogs and fens are often places to visit and to recreate. They re-connect us with nature and with history, often important in leisure and tourism, as backdrops for activities and visits, or the primary focus for the same. Frequently our images and expectations are based not on direct experience, but on observations, imaginations and writings of earlier visitors and commentators. Literary associations, place names, and even topographic names and descriptions may influence, positively and negatively, the desire to visit, to partake, and to experience. These perceptions and impressions are in part, acquired culturally over generations and over centuries. Furthermore, they interact intimately and directly with human psychological relationships to landscape and nature. Both reverence and fear influence these responses and over long periods as local residents were at risk from disease, death and natural disasters or catastrophes, and both the untamed nature and the fearsome strange people who lived there frightened visitors.

Today, fashions, art, science, transport and communications all play significant roles in the emerging sense of place and culture that now translate into the tourist landscape. These places are fearful as waste and wilderness. Yet being far from the madding crowd these wild areas draw the visitor to escape from the modern world to re-join nature and the cultural past. The reality may owe as much to fiction and careful packaging as it does to nature and history. Hollywood and the Victorian writers for example, draw visitors to the ancient heathland and Royal Forest of Sherwood as much as by any real understanding of the nature and history of the area. The accounts of travellers and commentators in Great Britain from the medieval to modern times help set the scene for contemporary images and associations. Recent research on the North Yorkshire Moors and Dales for the Yorkshire Tourist Board showed how visitors were still adversely affected by images of the '*Moors Murders*' (from the 1960s and a totally different geographical location), and even of the 1980s classic film '*American Werewolf in London*', the opening scenes of which are set in a bleak North Yorkshire moorland.

The assumed reality may owe as much to fiction and careful packaging as it does to nature and history. Hollywood and the Victorian writers for example, draw visitors to the ancient heathland and Royal Forest of Sherwood as much as by any real understanding of the nature and history of the area. The media in its diverse forms both feeds off these images, and develops, presents and event creates them. This may be from *Brontë Country* and *Last of the Summer Wine* in the Pennines of West Yorkshire, to *Heartbeat* on the North York Moors.

Ouseby (1990) and others have developed ideas of the relationships between people and tourism in relation to aspects of the English landscape, and in terms of nature and mountains in particular. This is something to be explored in more detail but this short paper is perhaps a small contribution to the theme. It is in part a spin-off from research on the cultural history of heaths, moors and bogs.

A fear of the unknown

The lessons of history are that wild nature, or nature perceived as wild is unexpected, unpredictable, disastrous, calamitous and fraught with the possibility of catastrophe. This fear is influenced by writers, topographers and travellers, and by both perceptions and facts. In Great Britain from the medieval to modern times, such issues have been explored and developed through the accounts of travellers and commentators. Images and reactions to nature and landscape occur in the literature of travel writers and of others. In 1624 in England, the anonymous author of *A Relation of a Short Survey of Twenty-six Counties* wrote in horror of the Lake District, and that it was '*...nothing but hideous hanging hills and great pooles, that in what respect of the murmuring noyse of those great waters, and those high mountainous, tumbling, rocky hills, a man would think he were in another world.*'

Figure 5. A fear of the unknown

Yet on the Continent, mountains had long been admired but not necessarily with enthusiasm but with awe. Conrad Gesner (1541) (In Hadfield, 1967): ... ' *...resolved for the future, so long as God grants me life, to ascend divers mountains every year .... What must be the pleasure, think you, what the delight of a mind rightly touched, to gaze upon the huge mountain masses for one's show, and, as it were, lift one's head into the clouds? The soul is strangely rapt with these astonishing heights*'.

Charles Cotton in 1681 in the Warden *of the Peak*: described the now second most popular National Park in the world, as '*Environ'd round with nature's shames and ills, Black heath, wild rock, bleak crags and naked hills.*' This is a transfer of visions and tastes from travellers. This was at odds with the formal and with God's creation and was linked to an abhorrence of the *Fall* from grace of Mankind.

Writers such as Joseph Addison (1701-3) were influential in both reflecting and determining taste in *Remarks on Several Parts of Italy in the Years 1701, 1702, 1703. 'I was most pleased with the beautiful prospect ....a more broken and interrupted scene, made up of an infinite variety of inequalities and shadowings, that naturally arise from an agreeable mixture of hills, groves and valleys.'*

Over the centuries, images of heathland and moor have been created by writers, artists and nowadays photographers. Some are factual and others are romanticised. The observers and portrayers themselves fall into distinct groups in terms of their objectives, backgrounds, and target audiences. Many accounts are the itineraries and diaries of gentlemen (and gentlewomen), travel writers, and topographers. These include the classic accounts of Daniel Defoe, Thomas Pennant, Samuel Johnson, and Dorothy Wordsworth *etc.* They observe and describe the landscapes through which they travel, the people they see, and those with whom they share hospitality. Their reactions to experiences and to environments helped forge the images and perceptions of their contemporaries, and still affect us today.

Daniel Defoe's description of the Peak District moors in 1724 (though often misquoted) influences reactions and expectation to this day. '*This, perhaps, is the most desolate, wild, and abandoned country in all England.*' He goes on to state that further north in the Pennines, around Lancaster the hills were '... *high and formidable only, but they had a kind of inhospitable terror in them ....all barren and wild, of no use or advantage to man or beast.*' Westmoreland is described as a '...*country eminent only for being the wildest, most barren and frightful of any* ...' In the south-west, Devon was '*at first sight, a wild, barren, poor country;...*'.

Figure 6. The Hound of the Baskervilles

Other writers such as novelists use these landscapes as backdrops for commentaries on specific communities and the lives of selected people. Thomas Hardy's novels of Dorset draw on personal knowledge of people, landscapes and events. As with Conan-Doyle's *Hound of the Baskervilles*, where the unfortunate convict on Dartmoor is mauled to death by the ferocious hound, and the villain then sinks to his slow death into the peat bog, they create an image that is burnt into the corporate imagination. The impact is deep and long lasting and reflected in contemporary reactions and images of these landscapes. Another way in which the public imagination is stimulated and fixed is through the vehicle of news reporting – in newspapers and magazines, and on television. Crimes on Cannock Chase and on Saddleworth Moor still affect people's sense of place even though transposed geographically many tens of kilometres across the landscape, from West Yorkshire to the North York Moors for example. The image of the '*Moors Murders*' generated a negative views of these landscapes that resonates across the corporate mind even today; and through this has a direct bearing on tourists and other visitors.

Figure 7. Brady and Hindley: the Moors Murderers

Diverse commentators have helped to create our images of these areas. W.H. Hudson and Richard Jefferies for example are two writers that followed Gilbert White in bringing insight of the countryside and nature to an increasingly urban population. This urban population has become the visitor and tourist now seeking to re-connect to the same experience. Gilbert White himself writing about his parish of Selborne set in a landscape of farmland, woodland, common and heath, gives a comforting feeling of stability and sensitivity in the lowland, pastoral setting. Not for White the murderer fleeing across the howling moor, or sinking slowly to his untimely end in a peat bog. Selborne has become a major visitor attraction, and White's main book *The Natural History of Selborne* (with its clever guise of letters penned to his friends and correspondents) is the fourth most published book in the English language, with well over 200 editions and translations.

These descriptions may be reassuring and comforting, or suggesting fear and trepidation, nature and challenge in the untamed wilderness. Travellers across Fowey Moor near Bodmin in Cornwall in the 1700s were advised to make their Wills prior to departure. The itinerant preacher John Wesley found his crossing of '*the great pathless moor*' extremely daunting and eventually found his way to Bodmin drawn only by the sound of the Town's evening curfew bell.

The impact of these writers and their descriptions, accurate or not, have had a huge influence on the perceptions and attitudes of visitors and others to these landscapes. In reviewing the classic work of Emily Brontë *Wuthering Heights*, Dante G. Rossetti wrote in 1847 that '*The action is laid in Hell………only it seems that the places and people have English names there.*' The windswept moors are the setting for this most tragic and stirring of love stories. Even the '*hero's*' name '*Heathcliff*' evokes the wild moorland landscape in which the story takes place. Their tempestuous relationship takes place within an equally wild and tempestuous environment. Brontë provides a brilliant example of scene setting in a novel and this evocation of the Yorkshire Moors, with their accompanying great houses is both dark and terrible.

However, it is important to realise that visitors are actually drawn to a place by fear and association, if merely to experience terror and loathing from the sanctuary of the hotel bar. So the late Victorian '*Hound of the Baskervilles*' by Sir Arthur Conan Doyle, created both fear of the place but also an irresistible attraction for future visitors to experience the bleak and horrific scene of the book, Dartmoor. *The Hound of the Baskervilles* written in 1902, sets the scene '*At Baskerville Hall on the grim moors of Devonshire, a legendary curse has ....*' and so it goes on. Both Conan Doyle's and Brontë's images have been further portrayed on television and in films to give an image of moors, heaths and bogs and wild , windswept landscapes, untamed, threatening and for many frightening. Moreover, you do not have to go there to know this; it is so deeply ingrained!

Figure 8. Watson and the great Grimpen Mire.

Out on the moor Watson hears the Hound for the first time. '*A long., low moan, indescribably sad, swept over the moor. It filled the whole air, and yet it was impossible to say whence it came. From a dull murmur it swelled into a deep roar and then sank back again into a melancholy, throbbing murmur once again.*' And later with Holmes: '*............. there rose out to the vast gloom of the moor that strange cry which I had already heard upon the borders of the great Grimpen Mire. It came with the wind through the silence of the night, a long, deep mutter, then a rising howl, and then a sad moan in which it died away.*'

Stapleton, the villain of *The Hound* says '*It is a wonderful place, the moor. You never tire of the moor. You cannot think the wonderful secrets which it contains. It is so vast and so barren, and so mysterious*'. Watson on the other hand describes '….. *that great Grimpen Mire, with little green patches everywhere into which one might sink and with no guide to point the track.*'

In his diary, Watson describes the '……*Bleak, cold, and shelterless moor*', and states that '*No one could find his way into the Grimpen Mire tonight.*' Then he describes their way through the bog: '…….. *green-scummed pits and foul quagmires which barred the way to the stranger. Rank reeds and lush, slimy water-plants sent an odour of decay and heavy miasmatic vapour into our faces, whilst a false step plunged us more than once into the dark, quivering mire, which shook for yards in soft undulations around our feet. Its tenacious grip plucked at our heels as we walked, and when we sank into it, it was as if some malignant hand was tugging us down into those obscene depths, so grim and purposeful was the clutch in which it held us.*' Another Conan Doyle hero Brigadier Gerard describes the landscape as: '*It is a bleak place this Dartmoor, wild and rocky - a country of wind and mist. I felt as I walked that it is no wonder Englishmen should suffer from the spleen.*'

Today, the scene is the Dartmoor National Park with around ten million tourism visitors a year. In contemporary landscapes heaths, commons, moors, bogs and fens are often places to visit and to recreate. For example, the North York Moors National Park receives around 1.4 million visitor days per year, and Exmoor the same. Fashions, art, science, transport and communications have all played significant roles in the emerging sense of place and culture that now translate into the tourist landscape. These places are fearful as waste and wilderness, yet being far from the madding crowd draw the visitor to escape from the modern world to rejoin nature and the cultural past.

Visions and images

The perceptions are of course dependent on the vision and the viewer. Wild areas of unkempt countryside did hold real threats and fears for the unknowing traveller. Until the 1700s and the early 1800s, they were also unbelievably difficult terrain to traverse. Added to these is the complication of language (in Wales, Ireland, Scotland and Cornwall) or at

Table 1. A first analysis of writers and their target audience

Writers	Contemporary Audience	Examples and comments
Novelists writing about the area in which they live or have lived.	Educated middle class readers of contemporary literature; in the towns and cities and in the big houses.	Emily Brontë; Thomas Hardy;
Novelists writing about the area but only acquainted through visiting.	Educated middle class readers of contemporary literature; in the towns and cities and in the big houses.	Arthur Conan Doyle; Walter Scott;
Commentators on the life and landscape of an area and usually resident within it.	Educated middle class readers of contemporary literature and initially their contemporaries with similar interests; in the towns and cities and in the big houses.	Gilbert White; W.H. Hudson;
Travel writers on a tour or similar visit specifically in order to commentate upon it.	Educated middle class readers of contemporary literature and particularly those now beginning to adventure out and start the move towards tours and tourism; in the towns and cities and in the big houses.	Thomas Pennant; Samuel Johnson; J. Boswell; William Cobbett;
Travel writers on a tour or similar visit writing as an incidental aspect of the visit.	Business and social colleagues, and perhaps family; generally educated middle class and mostly in the towns and cities, and in the big houses and their estates.	Dorothy Wordsworth;
Travel writers on a tour or similar visit concerned with their business, writing either as a report for a specific business purpose or as incidental to their visit; and commentators on the working landscape.	Business and social colleagues, and perhaps family, especially if they are involved in business; generally educated middle class and mostly in the towns and cities, and in the big houses and their estates; sometimes in military commissions.	Edmund Burt; Peter May; Arthur Young;

least dialect (in other remote heath and wetland areas of England and particularly places such as the English Fens), a further factor to put the traveller at a disadvantage and in a fearful state. Not only would this affect the feelings in terms of unease and vulnerability, but also it separated the traveller, observer, and perhaps writer from the native people.

In this respect, it is worth briefly considering who was writing and for whom the words were written. A casual inspection of relevant literature suggests a number of identifiable groupings, though some may fall into more than one category.

One of the issues here is that clearly with matters of literacy and of social order and distinction, in many cases these writers are on the outside looking in. This even applies when they are native to a region or to a specific area. The cultural, educational and social distinctions would have separated them from those more intimately involved in the day-to-day landscape. Also, and perhaps equally important is that their audience also lies well outside the landscape, culture and people of the heath, moor and bog. They are writing for their own, at least in terms of social standing and educational status.

Yesterday's cultural and literary landscape becomes today's tourism destination

As tourism developed, the audience clearly broadens to the present situation of mass tourism and mass communication. In many cases too, they wrote through the eyes of the romantic seeing a people and a landscape perhaps separated from the reality of the poor folk's daily grind. This is not always the case, and a half hour of Hardy's Egdon Heath in *Return of the Native* (1878) or *The Woodlanders* (1887) gives a very stark view of the life of the commoner and peasant in these subsistence environments. Yet the desperate landscape of the poor people portrayed so vividly by Thomas Hardy is now presented to the visiting public as '*Hardy Country*'. Much of the landscape has gone; heaths and commons lost to the plough or simply abandoned, yet the visiting public feel a connection to a rural and rustic past, through the visitor centre and teashop. Dorset is now a major tourism destination with historic market towns, seaside resorts and rolling landscape.

Another Conan Doyle hero Brigadier Gerard describes the landscape as: '*It is a bleak place this Dartmoor, wild and rocky - a country of wind and mist. I felt as I walked that it is no wonder Englishmen should suffer from the spleen.*' However, the 950 square kilometres of the Dartmoor National Park, with its 33,000 residents, attracts around 10 million tourist visitor days per year. The surrounding picturesque villages and hamlets, provide a welcome in food and accommodation, to comfort the image of the bleak, barren moor. Yet the backdrop is the vast expanse of wild landscape, in the case of the North York Moors for example, this amounts to around 490 square miles of moorland. The fear can now be safely experienced in comfort and at a distance.

The stark writings of Conan–Doyle and of Emily Brontë are just the stuff to attract visitors! The story was a huge success and led to *The Strand* magazine running to an unprecedented seven printings. It is also clear that the successes of stories and books such as this had, and still have, major impacts on visitors to an area. Loch Katrine in the Scottish Trossachs had particular association with and was the inspiration for, Walter Scott's poem The Lady of the Lake (1810). It sold 25,000 copies in only eight months and led to a dramatic increase in visitors to the Scottish Highlands (Hanley & Wildman, 2003).

An important point to consider is the extent to which these landscapes of moor, heath, common, marsh and bog, affected ordinary people until relatively recently, certainly, until the latter end of the Parliamentary Enclosures in the mid 1800s. They were widespread and abundant landscapes and figured centrally in the survival of ordinary working people. A key factor here is that they were far less important to the middle classes, to the educated and to the landowners. The middle class traveller, or resident in the rural landscape would be very aware of the moor, heath, common, and bog, but they were culturally separated from them. Perhaps here is the seed of the fear and loathing of the unknown.

Given this unpromising beginning, it is surprising in many cases how these landscapes have grown to be the tourism and recreational destinations of today. The Peak National Park of Defoe's description receives around 22 million or so day visitors per year, and the New Forest (with its ancient woods set amongst extensive heaths and bogs) has around 8 million. In fact today's tourists and day visitors love heaths and commons. This has been so much the case that many sites were badly damaged or even destroyed by insensitive holiday and recreational developments located in or on them during the 1970s and 1980s. More recent initiatives, such as at Centre Parcs and the Sherwood Forest Visitor Centre in Sherwood Forest, have been much more directly involved in safeguarding and enhancing the heathland heritage on which they are based. In popular tourist areas such as the North Norfolk Coast, the heaths that fringe the higher land above the coastal belt are very popular with visitors, campers, walkers and wildlife enthusiasts. Unlike many wooded landscapes, the heath offers the visitors a big sky and a distant gaze.

Much of the old landscape has gone, with heaths and commons lost to the plough, or simply abandoned, yet the visiting public feel a connection to a rural and rustic past, albeit through the visitor centre and tea shop.

Figure 9. Saddleworth Moor and the search for the Moors Murders victims.

Landscape and memory

The impact of literature is deep and long lasting and is reflected in contemporary reactions and images of these landscapes. However, another way in which the public imagination is stimulated and fixed is through the vehicle of news reporting, in newspapers and magazines, and on television. Descriptions may be reassuring and comforting, or suggest fear and trepidation, nature and challenge or threat in the untamed wilderness.

Emotional connections to landscapes

However, despite the attraction for some visitors, the big sky landscapes can also be frightening and intimidating, and the public's responses to moorlands and bogs are less certain. An experiment that I used to do with first year undergraduates at Sheffield Hallam University exemplifies this. Without any background briefing, I would take a new cohort of maybe forty to fifty students out onto Stanage Edge and Ringinglow Bog in Sheffield's Peak District National Park. I would give them around half an hour in small groups to reconnoitre the area and then ask for their feelings and impressions of this landscape. The response was very positive from around half the group, and most of these were individuals familiar with these landscapes. They were either local people, or perhaps with an interest in rock climbing or in walking. At least half the students did not like the area and found it '*bleak*', '*desolate*', '*empty*', '*cold*', '*too open*', '*hostile*' *etc*. My qualitative assessment was that the most damning comments were from students originating from urban, lowland areas. They found this a very uninviting and unfriendly landscape and were visibly shocked when told that it was the second most popular National Park in the world (after Mount Fuji in Japan).

In the lowland Fenlands, there are truly '*big sky*' landscapes, and this appeals to some but frightens or bores others. For some, they can impress beyond words and for others can depress beyond description. When Harry Godwin (later Sir Harry Godwin), Cambridge botanist and pioneer of palaeo-botanical approaches in ecology, began his twentieth-century studies, this issue was raised. His remark to a local fenman that he considered the Cambridgeshire area '*singularly flat*', prompted the reply: '*....any fool can appreciate mountain scenery, it takes a man of discernment to appreciate the Fens.*' This too affects how this area, its landscape, wildlife, and wilderness are considered and viewed over the centuries.

As Birks (1997) discusses for the Jamaica Inn near Bodmin Moor in Cornwall, much of the visitor experience is constructed by sets of signifiers brought together to construct a set of meanings. He points out of course that in practice many visitors are capable of constructing their own spheres of sociality and do not necessarily need them to be constructed on their behalf. How we the visiting public do this is complex and varying through time, space and through social evolution.

Questions Answered Limited examined the relationships to contemporary visitor and tourist perceptions through research on the North Yorkshire Moors and Dales National Parks. The Yorkshire Tourist Board commissioned this study, which gives a fascinating insight into contemporary awareness and responses to areas such as the North York Moors as visitor destinations. The study involved focus groups of a diverse socio-economic background and from different parts of England. It not only raises issues of response, image and awareness, but basic matters of geographic location! The North York Moors were described as barren with little formal interest other than the '*great outdoors.*' Some extracts and quotes exemplify this:

'*........Moors are very bleak. Bleakness, isolation if you want to be alone go to the Yorkshire Moors. If you want to get lost and never found, go to the Yorkshire moors*'.

'*No villages or accommodation or anything, I should imagine. It's all .... A bit more desolate isn't it*?'

'*Cornwall is very bleak and rugged and wild and wonderful .... which I tend to think of as the Moors*'.

'*.....really bleak places that are good for walking, windswept and weather beaten. ....but bleakness can be attractive at certain times of the year*'.

'*I think of heather and possibly walking but not much to go to, there wouldn't be much to go for.*'

'*The Moors would be purple, brown and bleak with long grass*'.

'*Land and the sky, stunning and dramatic!*',

'*Who would want to go to the Moors in the winter?!*'

'*Very, very bleak. You feel as if you're going for ever, even in the car and it's all the same scenery – seems endless.*'

'*......the countryside would go on and on for ever without much in it.*'

'......... *going out on those Moors ....are you going to come back? You could get lost.*'

Table 2. Some key words and phrases from the focus group interviews

Very wet and not very inspiring	Expanse of open space – freedom – walk around
Isolation, rugged but beautiful	Heavy rocks and bracken
Apprehensive .... but therapeutic	The fog!!
'Brontë country'	Lack of accommodation
Dangerous and rugged	Bad weather
Cold and chilly	Desolate – no trees
Not safe – fear of getting lost	Changeable weather
Slow, winding roads	Murders and werewolves
Wildly beautiful .... like a desert .... beautiful but harsh	Bleak, eerie, scary, rawness, poor weather
Awesome	Snow
Expansive	Cold and depressing
Harsh	Bleak and unwelcoming
The Moors Murders - Saddleworth	Murders on the moors
Less welcoming with cold rooms in the houses	Not safe
Scary	Apprehensive
Rustic, basic , lacking commercialisation	
In Summary: ***The Moors are dangerous, they are scary - and the weather's bad; and there's a lot of them!***	

A further issue to emerge from this research was the poor level of knowledge of the geographic location of areas such as the North York Moors within Yorkshire. This seemed good for the groups from Leeds and Nottingham, but very poor for group based in the south of England. This raises all sorts of issues in terms of branding and promotion. As noted earlier, some major barriers for visitor in the early twenty-first century were the 1960s 'Moors Murders'. Yet these were in a different area and a considerable distance away. However, this incident and the moorland scene from the 1980s film '*American Werewolf in London*', were both given as reasons not to visit the North York Moors.

What's in a name?

Name, identity and brand are clearly important for any site, area, or region that is or might be a tourism locale, or other visitor destination. Many place names are ancient in origin and often relate to land use or cultural occupation *etc*. Some of these are clearly developed over time to a particular brand or image. Others are straightforward impositions, and the most obvious is that of the '*Pennines*'; that vast tract of moor, heath, bog, and farmland that makes up the spine of England and Britain's first long distance footpath. Although the name '*The Pennines*' sounds authentic with a hint of Celtic origins, it is not. The name was the invention by writer Charles Bertram (1723-65) when he attributes it to the chronicles of Richard of Cirencester, something that he himself believed to have been forged. Until this time, there was no single name for the area. The name appears derived in part from the Apennines in Italy and whilst a deliberate fraud, the name has achieved resonance and is a hugely successful brand.

Discussion and Conclusions

Wetlands and associated areas of fens, bogs, heaths or moors, generate negative responses. This is an effect sealing the fate of many areas of rich wildlife habitat and cultural importance. William Gilpin, the pioneer of the '*Picturesque Landscape*' movement, writing in 1809 summed this up nicely when referring to the Cambridgeshire and Lincolnshire Fens some years earlier. He stated '*It is such a country as a man would wish to see once for curiosity; but would never desire to visit a second time. One view sufficiently imprints the idea. Indeed where there is but one idea, there can arise no confusion in the recollection.*'

Indeed, Gilpin pioneered the '*Picturesque Movement*' and triggered the idea that regions such as the hilly Peak District and the mountainous Cumbrian Lake District were beautiful places to visit and spiritually uplifting. In many ways, writing by Gilpin kick-started the '*Romantic Movement*', the Lakeland poets, and the colossal growth of tourism that followed. Prior to this, such upland areas were believed the works of the Devil to be avoided at all costs. The flipside of this was that many would-be visitors then avoided low-lying wetlands as malarial swamps and certainly not sufficiently picturesque for the refined visitor. The Fenlands were definitely not to be considered '*picturesque*'. The exceptions to this trend of avoidance were the Victorian naturalists, particularly entomologists who visited from Cambridge for rare Lepidoptera. Other visitors were fowlers and sportsmen; for them the picturesque nature was not a priority. Indeed, it is only now in the late twentieth and early twenty-first centuries that the tourist is once again returning to these big sky landscapes, and mostly thanks to the Royal Society for the Protection of Birds (RSPB), the National Trust, and others with their nature reserves.

Clearly, our perceptions of heath, moor, fen and bog influence our desire to experience and to visit. These are affected by the feelings and translations or constructions of feelings by those who have gone before. Work in North Yorkshire indicates some of the issues that then emerge for tourism and leisure managers with matters of branding, promoting and portrayal of these landscapes. Of course, that which is terrifying and desolate on the one hand can be inspiring and beautiful on the other. Perhaps feelings of fear and loathing are better from a tourism perspective than downright dull, boring and cold or wet. Fear can translate into excitement and a desire to visit and to partake.

Images of death and of murder still resound across our moorland and heathland landscapes. The moors murders are still a negative influence and may stop people coming to the North York Moors. This is a fear compounded by a lack of geographic knowledge – since the Moors Murders were in the West Yorkshire Pennines, a long way from the North York Moors.

However, Conan Doyle's image of the great Grimpen Mire runs deep. These feelings and responses have been with us for centuries. Thomas Preston touring Cornwall in 1821 described the landscape between Bodmin and Truro '*...the most dreary possible, a complete moor with scarce a dwelling visible, you may travel for miles over a swamp and see nothing but a few men at work at what is called 'streamwork'.*' He could almost have been one of the North York Moors focus group members.

In 1754, Caesar Thomas Gooch wrote that '*I have now seen a great deal of Cornwall and think it upon the whole a dismal country to live in .... the inland dwellings are a vast distance from the neighbours , everywhere surrounded with rocky mountains, and the prospects chiefly over barren lands.*' (Deacon, 1997). As a landscape portrayed by the emerging Romantic movement the same area could be described by Cyrus Redding in 1842, as '.... *the land of the wild, the picturesque and the imaginative.*' This was not a view shared by all, for example the Rev. Warner in 1809 had suggested that '...*however valuable it may be from a commercial pint of view, it can offer no claim to the praise of the picturesque or beautiful.*' (Deacon, 1997).

Very often, the images we have are not through our own eyes but those of some third party; maybe contemporary through books or the media, or perhaps from decades or centuries ago. It should also be remembered that beauty is of course in the eye of the beholder, and many things stem from this. Indeed, the type of response and emotion may vary with the individual, with social status, and with the time when the experience was had. This may result in something counter-intuitive to our modern, contemporary perception or response.

The itinerary of the French aristocratic travellers Alexandre de La Rochefoucauld and Maximilien Lazowski, in 1785-86, gives some insight into this (Scarfe, 2001). They were repelled at least at first by wild and uncultivated land – and especially in Scotland by poverty. North of Aberdeen they described as: '.... *The whole aspect of the country is so awful that the pleasure of travelling is nil... The views over the landscape are very melancholy, almost wholly uncultivated and extremely hilly*'. This compares with their impression of Leeds; ' .... *altogether a beautiful town*'. '*Three miles from Leeds you see it in the middle of a beautiful valley that contains both a canal and a river and is built over with immense numbers of houses; I think it's the richest view I ever remember looking at. This derives from the abundance of coal mines...*'

Travelling with the agricultural improver Arthur Young, they took tours, and described their opinions of the landscapes through which they passed. In Young's home area of Suffolk, now considered one of the most pretty and beautiful parts of England, François de La Rochefoucauld described Brandon in Suffolk:

'*I think the most driving, barren, and desolate tracts of land I ever met with, are crossed by the roads leading between Barton Mills and Brandon, and Bury and Brandon in Suffolk;*

but these are terribly loose and dry in their present state, and in a windy day fill the air with clouds of them. I instance these particularly, because I am fully persuaded that inclosing them and planting a certain quantity, would so far change the nature of the worst of them, as to make them fertile enough to yield good crops of corn, turnips, and grasses. Every one who is acquainted with those tracts of country, will be sensible what a prodigious improvement this would be.' The uncultivated lands of the Norfolk Brecks were '*twenty miles or so of wretched land we drove through that day*'.

Finally, how do people respond to the images and threats of wild and unknown nature? There are various possibilities applied through time and throughout the landscape. These are to move within the landscape, to re-build and protect, to abandon, and to avoid. As is always the case, the response is a compromise between the incentive to reside in an area, or to travel through a landscape, and in either case, to minimise or avoid risk or threat. The medieval fenlanders in England were well aware of the threat posed by inundation and flood, but these were productive environments and often areas, which were socially and politically safe and secure. The same dilemmas face people and communities across the globe today, and in light of global environmental changes, are ever more acute.

The dangers may be real and acute or they can be imaginary and driven by myth, ignorance or storytelling. Furthermore, how people respond to these issues and the messages presented, itself depends on their own direct experiences and on how they receive the messages. The experience and image may present differently for say a visitor to the North Yorks Moors from London, from New York, or from Japan. From the perspective of touristic development, this diversity of interaction is important and requires more detailed analysis. However, perhaps the mantra for a tourism destination might be to accept the diversity of message and response, but to assume that there is only one thing worse than being talked about, and that is not being talked about. In other words, if potential visitors to North Yorkshire, to the Peak District or to Dartmoor for example, have heard of the terrors that await them, then at least they know the location exists on the tourist map. They might then visit if only to be frightened and appalled. If they have never heard of the place then they certainly will not come.

Acknowledgements

Thanks to Joanna Royle of *Yorkshire Tourist Board* for access to their North York Moors perceptions study. *Questions Answered Ltd* are acknowledged as the originators of that primary research.

Bibliography and References

Adams, I.H. (ed.) (1979) *Papers on Peter May Land Surveyor 1749-1793.* Scottish History Society, Edinburgh.

Anon. (1629) *A discourse concerning the drayning of fennes and surrounded grounds in the sixe counteys of Norfolk, Suffolke, Cambridge, with the Isle of Ely, Huntington, Northampton and Lincolne.* London: 1629. Reprinted in 1647 under title: *The Drayner Confirmed, and the Obstinate Fenman Confuted.*

Anon. (1820) *The History and Antiquities of Thorne with some account of the drainage of Hatfield Chase.* S. Whaley, Thorne.

Anon. (2000) *The Yorkshire Dales & North Yorkshire Moors Branding and Perception Research.* Questions Answered Ltd, for Yorkshire Tourist Board, York.

Barnard, E.A.B. (1944) *A Seventeenth Century Country Gentleman (Sir Francis Throckmorton, 1640-80).* W. Heffer & Sons Ltd., Cambridge.

Birks, H. (1997) Jamaica Inn: the creation of meanings on a tourist site.
In: Westland, E. (ed.) (1997) *Cornwall - The Cultural Construction of Place.* Pattern Press (Publishers), Penzance, 137-142.

Blight, J.T. (1861) *A Week at the Land's End.* Longman, Green, Longman and Roberts, London.

Boswell, J. (1786) *Journal of a Tour to the Hebrides with Samuel Johnson.*

Bradley, A.G. (undated) *Highways and Byways in the Lake District.* Billing and Sons Ltd, London.

Bragg, M. (1983) *Land of the Lakes.* Secker and Warburg, London.

Camden, W. (1590) *Britannia Sive Florentissimorum Regnorum, Angliae, Scotiae, Hiberniae, Et Insularum Adiacentium.*

Cameron, K. (1961) *English Place-Names.* B.T. Batsford Ltd, London.

Cartwright, F.F. & Biddiss, M. (2004) *Disease & History.* Sutton Publishing, Stroud, Gloucestershire.

Conan Doyle, A. (1901-2) The Hound of the Baskervilles. *The Strand Magazine* (**August, 1901-April, 1902**). xi, [i], 110 pages.

Craig, W.J. (ed.) (1905) *The Oxford Shakespeare Complete works*. Oxford University Press, London.

Deacon, B. (1997) The hollow jarring of the distant steam engines: images of Cornwall between West Barbary and delectable Duchy. In: Westland, E. (ed.) (1997) *Cornwall - The Cultural Construction of Place*. Pattern Press (Publishers), Penzance, 7-24.

De Chateaubriant, A. (1927) *The Peat-Cutters*. (Translated by Robinson, F.M.), The Dial Press, New York.

De La Pryme, A. (1870) *The Diary of Abraham de La Pryme. The Yorkshire Antiquary*. Andrews & Co., Durham.

De La Pryme, A. (1699) Letters as quoted in Dinnin (1997). In: Van de Noort, R. & Ellis, S. (1997) *Wetland Heritage of the Humberhead Levels: An Archaeological Survey*. Humber Wetlands project, University of Hull, Hull.

Defoe, D. (1724-6) *A Tour Through the Whole Island of Great Britain*.

Dugdale, W. (1772) *The history of Imbanking and Draining of Divers Fens and Marshes, both in Foreign Parts and in this Kingdom, And of the Improvements thereby*. Second edition revised and corrected by Charles Nalson Cole, Printed by W. Bowyer and F. Nichols, London.

Giblett, R. (1996) *Postmodern wetlands, culture, history, ecology*. Edinburgh University Press, Edinburgh.

Gilpin, W. (1809) *Observations on Several Parts of the Counties of Cambridge, Norfolk, Suffolk, and Essex, also on Several Parts of North Wales; Relative Chiefly to Picturesque Beauty, in Two Tours, the Former Made in the Year 1769, the Latter in the Year 1773*. Published by his Trustees, printed in London.

Godwin, H. (1978) *Fenland: Its Ancient Past and Uncertain Future*. Cambridge University Press, Cambridge.

Hadfield, M (1967) *Landscape with Trees*. Country Life Ltd., London.

Hanley, K. & Wildman, S. (2003) *Ruskin's Romantic Tours 1837-1838*. Ruskin Library, University of Lancaster, Lancaster.

Harrison, K. & Rotherham, I.D. (2007) A memory re-discovered of South Yorkshire's fens: map-based reconstruction of the region's former wetlands. *The Yorkshire Naturalists' Union Bulletin*, **48**, 1-8.

Heathcote, J.M. (1876) *Reminiscences of Fen and Mere*. Spottiswoode and Co., London.

Hills, R.L. (1967) *Machines, Mills & Uncountable Costly Necessities. A short history of the drainage of the fens. The Drainage of the Fens*. Goose & Son, Norwich.

Humphreys, M. (1997) *Malaria: 'Evil' Air and Mosquitoes*. In: Kiple, K. (ed.) (1997) *Plague, Pox & Pestilence. Disease in History*. Weidenfeld & Nicholson, London.

Johnson, S. (1775) *Journey to the Western Islands of Scotland.*

Lowenthal, D. (1985) *The Past is a Foreign Country*. Cambridge University Press, Cambridge.

Mabey, R. (1986) *Gilbert White. A biography of the naturalist and author of The Natural History of Selborne*. J.M. Dent, London.

Miller, S.H. & Skertchly, S.B.J. (1878) *The Fenland Past and Present*. Longmans, Green, and Co., London, and Leach and Son, Wisbech.

Moody, N. (1997) *Poldark Country and National Culture*. In: Westland, E. (ed.) (1997) Cornwall - The Cultural Construction of Place. Pattern Press (Publishers), Penzance, 129-136.

Morton, H.V. (1927) *In Search of England*. Methuen and Co. Ltd., London.

Mullins, R. (1998) *The Inn on the Moor – A History of Jamaica Inn*. PR Publishing (Cornwall).

Ousby, I. (2002) *The Englishman's England. Taste, Travel and the Rise of Tourism*. Pimlico, London.

Pryme, G. (Edited by Alicia Bayne) (1870) *Autobiographic Recollections Of George Pryme Esq., M.P.*. Deighton, Bell and Co, Cambridge.

Pryor, F. (1991) *Flag Fen. Prehistoric Fenland Centre*. B.T. Batsford Ltd., London.

Roberts, C. & Cox, M. (2003) *Health & Disease in Britain. From Prehistory to the Present Day*. Sutton Publishing, Stroud, Gloucestershire.

Rollinson, W. (ed.) (2000) *William Gell - A Tour in the Lakes 1797*. Smith Settle Ltd., Otley.

Room, A. (1988) *Dictionary of British Place Names*. Bookmart Ltd edition 1995.

Rotberg, R.I. (ed.) (2000) *Health and Disease in Human History: A Journal of Interdisciplinary History Reader*. The MIT Press, Cambridge.

Rotherham, I.D. (1999) Peat cutters and their landscapes: fundamental change in a fragile environment. *Landscape Archaeology and Ecology*, **4**, 28-51.

Rotherham, I.D. (2004) *Commentary and Creation - writers on life and travel in heath, moor and bog*. Paper in: Conference Proceedings - Tourism and Literature, Travel, Imagination and Myth Conference Handbook, International Research Conference, Harrogate, United Kingdom, 22-26 July 2004, Centre for Tourism and Cultural Change. Robinson, M. & Picard, D. (eds) ISBN 1 84387 085 3.

Rotherham, I.D. (2008) *The Importance of Cultural Severance in Landscape Ecology Research.* In: Editors: Dupont, A. & Jacobs, H. *Landscape Ecology Research Trends*, ISBN 978-1-60456-672-7, Nova Science Publishers Inc., USA, Chapter 4, pp 71-87.

Rotherham, I.D. (2008) *Floods and Water: A Landscape-scale Response.* In: Rotherham, I.D. (ed.) (2008) *Flooding, Water and the Landscape.* Wildtrack Publishing, Sheffield, 128-137.

Rotherham, I.D. (2008) *Landscape, Water and History.* In: Rotherham, I.D. (ed.) (2008) *Flooding, Water and the Landscape.* Wildtrack Publishing, Sheffield, 138-152.

Rotherham, I.D. (2009) *Peat and Peat Cutting.* Shire Publications, Oxford.

Rotherham, I.D. (2010) *Yorkshire's Forgotten Fenlands.* Pen & Sword, Barnsley.

Rotherham, I.D. (2013) *The Lost Fens: England's Greatest Ecological Disaster.* The History Press, Stroud.

Rotherham, I. D. & Harrison, K. (2006) *History and ecology in the reconstruction of the South Yorkshire fens: past, present and future.* Proceedings of the IALE Conference, *Water and the Landscape: The Landscape Ecology of Freshwater Ecosystems*, 8-16.

Scarfe, N. (1988) A Frenchman's Year in Suffolk: French impressions of Suffolk life in 1784. *Suffolk Records Society*, **Volume XXX**, The Boydell Press, Woodbridge, Suffolk, England, 226 + xxxvii.

Scarfe, N. (1995) *Innocent Espionage: The La Rochefoucauld Brothers Tour of England in 1785.* The Boydell Press, Woodbridge, Suffolk, England.

Scarfe, N. (2001) *To the Highlands in 1786.The inquisitive journey of a young French aristocrat.* The Boydell Press, Woodbridge.

Shakespeare, W. (1905) *King Lear, II, iv, 169.* Oxford Standard Authors, Oxford.

Simmons, A. (ed.) (1998) *Burt's Letters from the North of Scotland as related by Edmund Burt. First published 1754.* This edition by Birlinn Limited, Edinburgh.

Simpson, W.D. (1969) *Portrait of the Highlands.* Robert Hale, London.

Smallhorn, T. (1987) *Most Brute and Beastly Shire.* Richard Kay, Boston, Lincolnshire.

Smout, C. (2000) *Nature Contested - environmental history in Scotland and Northern England since 1600.* Edinburgh University Press, Edinburgh.

Taylor, M. (1987) *Thorne Mere and the Old River Don.* Ebor Press.

Tomlinson, J. (1882) *The Level of Hatfield Chace and Parts Adjacent.* John Tomlinson, Doncaster.

Wainwright, A. (1986) *A Pennine Journey –The Story of a Long Walk in 1938.* Michael Joseph, London.

Westland, E. (ed.) (1997) *Cornwall - The Cultural Construction of Place.* Pattern Press (Publishers), Penzance.

White, G. (1788-9) *The Natural History of Selbourne.*

Woolley, B. (2004) *The Herbalist: Nicholas Culpeper and the fight for medical freedom.* HarperCollins, London.

Wrangham, C.E. (ed.) (1983) *Journey to the Lake District from Cambridge 1779. A diary written by William Wilberforce. Undergraduate of St. John's College, Cambridge*. Oriel Press London.

Young, A. (1772) *Political Essays*. (Re-printed 1970 by Research Reprints Inc., New York) W. Strahan and T. Cadell, The Strand, London.

Young, A. (1804) *General View of the Agriculture of the County of Norfolk.* The Board of Agriculture, London.

Young, A. (1811) *On the Husbandry of Three Celebrated British Farmers: Messrs Bakewell, Arbuthnot, and Ducket*. Publisher not stated.

Figure 10. A witch by Denys James Watkins-Pitchford

Between the Atlantic and the Mediterranean

Responses to Climate and Weather Conditions throughout History

Edited by *Cristina Joanaz de Melo, Ana Isabel Queiroz, Luís Espinha da Silveira and Ian D. Rotherham*

Proceedings of the conference held at Faculdade de Ciências Sociais e Humanas, Universidade NOVA de Lisboa, Lisbon, 4th-5th May 2012

Published in 2013 by Wildtrack Publishing, Venture House, 103 Arundel Street, Sheffield, S1 2NT, UK.

www.ingramcontent.com/pod-product-compliance
Ingram Content Group UK Ltd.
Pitfield, Milton Keynes, MK11 3LW, UK
UKHW050614260726
13967UKWH00008B/2870